NOT Unto
Death

Lonnette A. Liggins Collazo

Fulton Books
Meadville, PA

Published by Fulton Books 2025

Cover Design Credit: Lorah A.

ISBN 979-8-88505-691-5 (paperback)
ISBN 979-8-89427-135-4 (hardcover)
ISBN 979-8-88505-692-2 (digital)

Printed in the United States of America

DEDICATION

I would like to sincerely dedicate this book to and thank the following people for the various things they did (some unknowingly) that helped me along this journey: this was at times I thought to be an impossible and hopeless personal journey in which those I thought would/should be there for me weren't; but God sent so many others: ***often complete strangers,*** to stand beside me and support me!

- My husband, Efrain Collazo Rodriguez, who remains a ***constant*** source of love, inspiration, encouragement, support and motivation along this journey. I could ***not*** have made it without him. I ***always*** felt his presence even when he was unable to physically be with me! You ***complete*** me!
- My children: Jessica Collazo Guzman (and son-in- law, Eduardo Guzman) who helped in so many ways and were both great sources of support and motivation when we had no one else; also, our son.
- My late fur baby "Zoe" who slept by my head for nearly 2 years to tell me something was wrong and

waited until after I got back from being away for 2 months for my cancer treatment and took her last breath in my arms shortly after I returned.

- My current fur babies: Gracie, Stormy (that during hard times were literally my reason for getting out of bed some days) and our newest fur baby and so amusing: Juanita as well as the late "Picah", "Snapple" and my grandpups: "Nova" (Gammy's Baby) so loving to her Gammy and of course "Rogue" (Gammy's wild child).

- The surgeon who *listened* to God's Voice and saved my life.

- Stephanie Bazille (head of my Proton Radiation team at MD Anderson) and her amazing staff for effectively completing the 35 rounds of radiation. They showed me so much professionalism and compassion and kept me motivated as I went through the 2 months of cancer treatment unaccompanied.

- Former Congressman John Duncan Jr. (and his amazing staff) of Knoxville, TN whose passion and respect for our military was so touching. They worked diligently and successfully to get Tricare (Military Insurance) to execute an "Exception to Policy" to keep me off a feeding tube after numerous denials.

- The Staff of Southeast Oral Surgery in Knoxville, TN (Dr. Troy Randall Napier D.M.D., Maggie Kirkland, Susan Lara, Michelle Tracy, and Raven Trimble) who helped me with documentation for letters of support to my insurance and Congressman, listened to me cry and encouraged me so much along the way as I continued to lose teeth, weight and hope! I can never repay you for the acts of kindness you showed me and my family.
- Dr. William Smartt D.D.S of Knoxville, TN who made and installed the dental implants and worked so hard to make them beautiful and greatly raised my self-esteem and gave me the ability to eat again.
- My neurologist, Dr. Karen Mullins, D.O. of Alcoa, TN, (and Andrea) who worked diligently to get me approved for preventive migraine treatments and effective medications for headaches and still asks about the status of this book that I have been writing for years at *every* visit/treatment!
- My Primary Care Provider, Dr. Kaneez Leonard Bowden (nurse Christine) M.D. of Knoxville, TN, and staff who continue to manage my care and **really** listens to ensure that I get the proper testing to ensure I remain cancer and tumor free and healthy overall. If she doesn't know the answer, she researches until she does or facilitates referrals.

- Dr. Harold Silver M.D. (Gastroenterologist) of Knoxville, TN who saved my life after *I lost nearly 2/3 of my total blood supply* due to a tear in my intestine that caused massive internal bleeding as well as his love and respect of our United States military.
- Khady Sady, who always does my hair to eliminate migraines and make me feel beautiful. She has become like another daughter to me and always encouraged me with my goal to write this book
- Hope Alexander Gillespie: my friend, sister in Christ and the person who unknowingly at the time (over 40 years ago), introduced me to my husband, best friend and "Knight in Shining Armor!"
- My cousin Darlene Smith who consistently checks on me, always prays for and encourages me and her many acts of kindness!
- Kathy White (and staff) of 'The Soup Kitchen Express" of Knoxville, TN who unknowingly provided nourishment to my body when I couldn't do it for myself.
- Pamela Hofe: who was the catalyst to me discovering me "peaceful place" Band.
- Jim Morris: who made me realize my strengths and taught me the *true* power and rewards of motivation and perseverance and without know-

ing, helped me take/stay the right course when I reached those "forks in the road!"

- Cathedral of Grace family in Decatur, GA: Bishop Darrius key and his wife, Pastor Jacqueline Key (whom I have known since kindergarten) who continue to check on me, encourage, support and pray for me. They have shown me that geographical space has **no** power in **true** worship and love for one another.

- Hal and Edie Kinney of GSE Karaoke who provided an outlet and atmosphere of fun, support and healing through music and gave me the courage to overcome my fear of standing/singing before people and in return allowed me to meet some wonderful people in which some have become great friends.

- A plethora of friends and other medical staff who all played significant roles in both my mental and physical survival and this project completion. (I apologize to anyone unknowingly not listed).

- The Pittsburgh Steeler Organization (in which I had been cheering for since age 4)! They learned of my journey through efforts of our awesome daughter and sent me a plethora of team memorabilia to include a terrible towel, bracelets, a game ball (signed by The Rooneys, **every** player, **every** coach and *every* coordinator that year) as well as an inspiring letter of encouragement.

- A *huge* 'Thank You" to Brittany Goldsmith for her amazing heart of compassion. Thank you from *both* my husband and I for pushing through an unfavorable mess you inherited and going *exceedingly well beyond* your "scope of duties" to encourage me and fight to have this book completed and published. You were *literally* my eyes and voice at times and have *restored* my faith in humanity.

- A very special and sincere thanks to the people who rejected, abandoned, used and mistreated me and showed me who you *really* were: "You thought you broke me, but *instead* you forced me to lean harder on the Lord and that made me *"STRONGER"!*

- For those of you who intentionally or mistakenly counted me out… *THAT WAS YOUR BIGGEST MISTAKE!*

- To anyone and everyone that is going through something, I hope you are inspired and blessed by the reading of this book and my various testimonies.

REMEMBER GOD ALWAYS HAS THE FINAL SAY!

PREFACE

When I was about 5 1/2 years old, I can recall on a few occasions in which my parents and another couple (friends of theirs) would go out after midnight and raid a cornfield or two and take a couple of pillowcases of fresh corn to both help supplement our sometimes-limited food supply and they would always share with a few others in that same situation.

I know they thought I was too young to notice and of course they tried to hide it from us because no matter if it does appear as a "Robin Hood" deed, it was stealing and wrong!

On one of these occasions, I was to learn another valuable lesson:

One night I pretended to have my nightclothes on and to be fast asleep but that was not the case at all! In fact, I knew they were going on a "cornfield mission" that very night and I had already plotted or had my "game plan" in action!

They would always use our family station wagon little did they know that right after they checked to see if we were all asleep, I sprang from my bed fully dressed and ready to witness their mission. I snuck out the back door and went and hid in the third-row seating. When they were almost to their destination, I sprang up from the very back and yelled, "Surprise!" I'm sure that almost gave my dad his first heart attack as he swerved and eventually regained control of the vehicle and pulled over to the shoulder of the road.

After some scolding and discussion, they agreed that I could go as long as I laid down and remained in the car. They got to the cornfield and upon exiting the vehicle they once again ordered me to keep the doors locked for, they would only be a few minutes or so they thought.

A few minutes after they left, I got scared, it was so dark and silent out there. I exited the car and headed towards the cornfield not realizing how easy it was to get lost in a cornfield in broad daylight let alone in the darkest of night. I could hear movement in the cornfield as I continued to walk deeper and deeper into it. Abruptly, reality hit me, and I realized that I was lost. Eventually fear took over and I began to cry and call for my father to come and get me.

After a few attempts he heard me and told me to stay where I was and that it was going to be okay. He told me to sing my ABC's until he got to me. I could hear movements getting closer to me as I obeyed and stood still and sang. My father once again told me to stay still, don't move and keep singing.

Within a few minutes (that felt more like an eternity) he found me and dropped his pillowcase of corn and extended his arms around me to embrace and comfort me and told me that everything was going to be okay. When I felt his presence and calmed down, I knew that I was safe, and no harm could come to me. Then he picked up his pillowcase and used his free hand to hold my hand and led me to safety. I didn't even get a whooping that night.

Today, I say to you that may be in a "cornfield" of fear and trouble: Call on "The Father", stand still, sing and wait until "Our Father" finds you, extends his Hand and leads you to safety even through our disobedience.

I never understand when I hear people say, "When they found God." For it is us that become lost until we cry out to "Our Father!" He's **always** around just waiting for us to call upon Him!

Chapter 1

It was just another typical day in March 2010, well, as typical as the past several months had been for me. For some reason, my blood pressure, which had always been low to normal, had elevated to nearly stroke range; and after months of seeing various doctors and going through various tests, including wearing heart monitors, blood work, etc., nothing had changed. Or so I thought.

So I was getting ready for work, and as I headed into my bathroom for my final stage of my morning routine before my thirty-plus-mile commute, all dressed and teeth brushed, I got nothing left to do but fluff out my hair and put on a little makeup. By this time, I had my morning routine down to a science. I knew exactly when I had to leave to avoid the school zones and the traffic jams heading into Oak Ridge. I guess I should, I had been doing it for over ten years and most of it while single-parenting my two kids (and for three of those years, my nephew) while my husband was being deployed back-to-back to back-to-back...(okay, you get it) to the Middle East.

Oh yeah, where was I? Ah yes, the final steps to "Operation Mommy Heads Out to Conquer the Day and

1

Bring Home that Pay!" So I dumped my cosmetic bag onto the bathroom vanity. As I looked up to put my moisturizer on, I felt a little light-headed, so I sat on the stool and took a deep breath and continued on with my routine. Next up was a light coat of foundation. Done. Now time for eyeliner. What in the name of Jesus? Was this big mirror playing tricks on me? No way was the pupil in my right eye moving back and forth involuntarily at the speed of light! I was not seeing this!

Okay, first instinct was to take a deep breath, and second instinct was to close my eyes, open, and look again. Oh God. It was still doing it! No, I did not go into full panic mode yet! I just slapped myself on the right side of the head until it stopped! That always works, right?

Okay, here it went: *slap, slap, slap* and I opened my eyes. It was still doing it. I tried again, *slap, slap, slap* and I opened my eyes. It was still doing it. Okay, one more time, but this time, harder: *slap, slap, slap*. Then I opened my eyes. Oh my God, thank You. It had stopped! Wait a minute…why did I have double vision in that eye now? This might be the time to panic! Just saying.

Chapter 2

S o there I was sitting in the ophthalmologist's office of a huge practice that I had never been to before, but I called, and they could get me in that same morning and accepted my insurance. I had cleared my early morning schedule at work and told them I would be in around lunchtime.

Are you kidding me? How many forms did they expect me to fill out with this off and on double vision? No problem. I counted each form by flipping them facedown in the empty chair next to me just to make sure I wasn't seeing double, no such luck. I completed what seemed like the book of Psalms and went up to the front desk and turned in the forms. They returned my forms of ID and insurance card back to me. Funny how these doctors' offices seem to hold these items hostage.

All I kept thinking was why today? My son who did not like to be fussed over had been working full-time and going to college full-time as well and had just told me and his dad the night prior that he was graduating this evening and not just graduating, but graduating valedictorian and please do not make a big fuss over it. Yeah, right! I was not on social media at that time, but I had texted or called more people in those few hours than I had in years! I couldn't wait to get to work so I could brag to everyone there. I had already figured out my strategy. Somewhere around the microwave or Xerox machine, I would mention that I had to leave early today, and when asked why, *buh blam!* Let the bragging begin.

My thoughts were interrupted when I heard them mispronouncing my name, as 99 percent of the population that I have encountered does. I proceeded to the back with a technician who pretty much asked me the reason for my visit and everything else that was already on those magazine-thick layers of forms I had already filled out. Nonetheless, I smiled and answered every question as politely and accurately as I could. I then underwent a series of eye examinations and various tests and then was walked down to another room in which I was told the doctor would be in with me shortly to discuss the findings.

In case you were wondering, I had not called or told my husband yet. Yeah, I thought I was superwoman mainly because I had to be for most of my life. Always working wherever we were stationed whether it be Europe two times or anywhere in the United States as well as during all his combat deployments, border patrols, peace keeping missions, and training drills and never any family around. Not that that would make a difference. They were never supportive of me, and that was just how things were and unfortunately would remain. I escaped my hometown as early as I could to create a place of peace, love, and success. I guess I was and possibly always will be resented for that.

It makes me reflect on a church prayer service that I attended about 3 years after my brain surgery. I had been through so much physically, emotionally, spiritually, surgically, financially, and any other "lly" you could think of that the night prior to that service, God spoke to my heart and spirit and told me to write down everything that I was holding onto that was keeping me from healing in those areas and stealing my peace. I obeyed and went to find paper and a pen. As I opened a drawer on my bedroom dresser in search of a pen, I found a beautiful gift box that had come with a necklace and earring set that I had purchased many years prior. When I completed writing down everything, I folded the papers and stuck them inside the gift box and stuck it in my purse. The next evening during prayer service God told me to take the box to the altar and leave it and that is what I did. It was symbolic of me releasing all of it to God to handle.

So about twenty-five minutes later, the doctor came into the room and introduced himself. He told me that all the tests showed that I had perfect vision, just a slight astigmatism in one eye which was normal for age forty-three, but it looked like I just had a case of dry eye. He spun back on his stool and over to a cabinet and pulled out some drops and then *pitched* them to me. He told me to make an appointment for a two-week follow up and to be sure to use those drops and proceeded to head for the door.

I don't know what got into me. It could have been the months of going through what seemed every kind of doctor or test there was with no diagnosis, maybe his lack of bedside manner, or maybe I was just pissed at him for not taking me seriously and feeling like I had not been taken seriously by any of the other doctors I had seen over the last year and a half. My guess was it was all of the above! I grabbed him by his lab coat, as he was attempting to leave and said, "No, Sir, something is wrong, and I need you to do your job!"

He seemed a bit taken back as well as I. Did I really just do and say that? Next thing I knew he came back in and shut the door and told me to sit down. At this point, I didn't know if he was actually going to take me seriously or if he was just stalling me until security arrived. I was thinking there was a panic button in that room or on his person that he had activated.

Nonetheless, I did what he said and awaited my fate. He shined a pocket light into both of my eyes and then had me perform some eye muscle/nerve tests, and then he sat down and went, "Hmm." Just the words you want to hear a doctor say, but if he could tell me what was wrong, I would be glad to get on the road to recovery or so I thought. Then he said, "You have sixth nerve palsy. I've never seen it in anyone so young."

So I was waiting for an explanation of what that was and how to cure it. Come on, unless you had some profound medical background or knew someone with it, it was not something you hear every day. "Hey, Lonnette, how's it going? Okay, ole sixth nerve palsy kind of acting up today!" So the expression on my face must have said it all; my daughter often tells me this. I was just looking at him, and then he proceeded to tell me that sixth nerve palsy is when the sixth optic nerve becomes damaged usually, due to suddenly elevated blood pressure, but once the blood pressure returns to normal, the nerve heals itself.

"Well, that's just dandy," I said to him.

But there was just one thing: no one could find the reason for my sudden rise in blood pressure. There was neither history of high blood pressure in my family nor when I was morbidly obese at 331 lbs just a few years earlier. Even then, my blood pressure was normal. Now it was stroke range! Now I was sitting there at a proud 165 lbs, exercising every day (rain or shine), new lifestyle, etc., and my blood pressure went bonkers now! What gives?

His answer was, 'These things happen."

I told him, with all due respect, I needed answers, and I needed him to perform whatever tests to get those answers for me. My frustration level had probably surpassed my blood pressure levels at this point. He then stated to me in the most condescending level I had been spoken to in some time, "I'm sure there is nothing wrong, but to put your mind at ease, I will just order a MRI for behind your eye as well as a brain MRI." He said to take the form over to the next building, and they would be waiting for me, and he would see me in two weeks to see how those drops for my dry eye worked out for me. He even gave me the old smoking guns and clicking action. It was obvious that he was convinced that his original diagnosis of dry eye was the culprit.

As I began heading to the other building I recalled from a couple weeks earlier what was a strange incident that occurred: I was doing my normal walking laps around the pond at work when just before the ¼ mile mark on the first bench I noticed a very old, Caucasian lady. She seemed to have appeared from nowhere. As I passed her, I smiled and she said "Hello" and I smiled back and noticed that she was looking down at a really old book. I continued on around the pond and as I was approaching her for my second lap around, she said "Nice day, isn't it?" Something told me to go sit beside her (I've always enjoyed the company of older people). I told her it was a very nice day and proceeded to tell her my name and ask her what her name was. She smiled and continued to turn the pages of what I was able to see was a very old photo album filled with very old black and white photos that were beginning to yellow around the edges.

I thought she didn't hear me so I asked for her name again. She once again didn't say but began showing me the photos and saying how much she missed her husband who were in the photos she was showing me as I looked at the photos she shared the story behind each one of them.

After a while I realized that time was getting away from me and I told her that I had to get back to work. I also told her that I enjoyed talking with her and hoped that I would get to see her again on my next daily walk. I once again told her my name and asked for hers. Once again she didn't reply. She only looked me in the eye, and said, "You know everything is going to be alright!" I got up and took a few steps and turned around to ask her what she meant by that remark and she was gone!

There was nothing around my workplace but another badge secured building that was several feet away, the pond, and further down the road was an apartment complex that was being built. Plus she appeared to be 80 or 90 years old! There was no way she could've moved that quickly and I was wide awake and walking definitely not dreaming. It is now that I truly believe that she was an angel that was sent to warn and assure me.

Chapter 3

So off to the next building I went. I reported to the front desk and gave them the MRI orders. They in return asked for my identification and insurance card. Oh no, the dreaded clipboard. I sat down to fill out these forms. Not as bad as the ones earlier; they were about as thick as the book of Jude maybe even Obadiah.

A few minutes later, my name was mispronounced for the second time this morning as I was called to the back. I informed the technician that I had a couple more forms to complete. She said, "No problem. You can get to those later just as long as you sign the ones permitting us to bill your insurance and understanding who the responsible party is for any balance remaining." That seems to be the real priority these days. Sad…but true!

I smiled and continued to walk with her to a small dressing/locker room area. She advised me to remove my jewelry, hair accessories and clothing (keeping only my panties on) and store them in one of the lockers, put on one of the facility gowns, and hang on to the key. I would be sitting in another waiting area with others who had the same privilege of wearing matching "gowns of shame." I followed her directions to the tee, and I was so proud when I could wrap the gown around me twice. I even gave it a sassy side bow. After what seemed like a season changed, my names were mispronounced again, and I was led down a long quiet hallway and into a door, which opened to an eerie room with a slab instead of a cot and all sorts of equipment I had never seen before. Little did I know then that I would make this type of machine's acquaintance nearly ninety times and counting over the next 15 years and counting!

Chapter 4

As I entered the room, something within me changed or felt different. I really couldn't explain it. It wasn't fear even though the room did look like something from a science fiction movie. I had no idea what they were about to do to me, perhaps clone me? (That would be cool. I would send the clone to work and have her clean the house and all that good stuff while I...okay, I was back.) A girl could dream! Well, like I was saying, something within me happened; and I knew that one way or another, when I left this room, my life was going to change. God had already dropped that into my spirit.

I was led to what looked like an autopsy table with some sort of time travel machine hood around it. If it were a time travel device, I don't think I would ever travel back unless it was to see my mom or grandpa one last time... Okay, I would probably repeat my high school band years for sure, as well as the first time I laid eyes on my husband of nearly 39 years presently and met over 41 years ago. I was told that the doctor had asked for MRIs with and without contrast. First would be the ones without contrast. I was also told to remain perfectly still and given a panic button to push in case I needed it.

I am sure that you had figured out by now that I had never had an MRI, only X-rays three years earlier when I had been hit full frontal head-on by a reckless driver who was speeding in a borrowed vehicle in the rain with her infant child around one of the curviest roads in the area. Why did I emphasize borrowed? Well, let's just say that I had to hire an attorney because I was given false information at the scene. The attorney discovered she had totaled out her new Lexus just two weeks prior to totaling out my vehicle and nearly me.

Yeah, I sustained fourteen fractures. Praise God that her baby was fine and picked up at the scene by a relative. The poor "repeat offender of wrecks" driver sustained a knee abrasion, and the ambulance transported her first. I had enough time between ambulances to call my husband at work and tell him what happened, only for him to drive twenty minutes to the scene and wait another ten minutes for the ambulance to arrive for me. He even helped load me in. Well, that was a story for another time or maybe another book. Keep in mind, I have been through some stuff!

Okay, back to the MRI. So I was given some earplugs, and once again, I was told to remain perfectly still and reminded about the panic button. I felt myself being eased into and, later, sucked into what seemed a giant Bissell vacuum. There were all sorts of noises, bells, and alarms going off. I just closed my eyes and tried to concentrate on my son's graduation later that day. My thoughts were interrupted by a voice coming through the speakers of the machine asking me if I had a follow-up appointment scheduled with the doctor, and I said, "Yes, in two weeks."

The tests continued on. Eventually, I was slid back out; and this time, an IV was inserted into the top of my right hand, and some red fluid began to rush through my body. It felt warm because I was really cold and kind of shaking at this point. I was offered a warm blanket and gladly accepted. Then back into the machine I went. This time, for some reason, I was thinking about the movie "Honey, I Shrunk the Kids." I knew the mind was a crazy thing. It would be ironic that after losing 170 lbs, I would be shrunk even smaller. Once again, my thoughts were interrupted by the same voice, "Hmm, do you have a follow-up scheduled with the doctor?" I replied again, "Yes, Ma'am, in two weeks."

The tests continued on for a while longer and then complete silence for several minutes. The table rolled out, and the technician gave me the key to my locker and told me to get dressed and that was all that was needed. I thanked her, and once again, she asked me if I had a follow-up scheduled with the doctor. Yet again, I replied, "Yes, Ma'am, in two weeks."

As I gathered my things from the locker and got dressed, I was thinking either this was the most forgetful person in the world or something was **wrong**.

I went straight to work and, of course, bragged about my son's status at his upcoming graduation later that evening. We all met at the house to get dressed. My son had to be there early; but my husband, daughter, and I and, oh yeah, my husband's brother who was running from street trouble in Puerto Rico was visiting/living with us. (Another story for another day/book?)

We were all loaded up in the car and headed downtown at almost the worst time of day for the graduation ceremony when my phone rang. I answered it, and it was the ophthalmologist's office calling me. On the other end, a representative was asking if I could come and meet with the doctor today for he would be there a couple more hours. I told her that I already had a follow-up appointment with him in two weeks. She replied, "He really needs to see you today." I politely told her that we were en route to our son's college graduation, which he was valedictorian (another opportunity to brag and be so proud of), and I was not missing that for anything! She said that she understood and asked if I could make or clear some time to come in tomorrow. We agreed on 11:30 a.m. the following day. I hung up the phone, and my husband who was driving asked who was on the phone. I told him the ophthalmologist's office just needed me to make a follow-up appointment.

We proceeded towards downtown. My phone rang again; this time, it was one of my brothers who was, once again, canceling at the last minute, stating that he would not be able to make it to his nephew's graduation…whomp wa…wa, wa whomp, whomp. I had heard it all too many times before from five of six of my siblings (two brothers and three sisters) when it came to anything to support me (including when I sustained the fourteen fractures and **not one** came to visit or help me) or my family. Except for one of my sisters who made sure to at least make it to both of my children's high school graduations but still for some reason, *never* in my times of need! (To be continued.)

We finally arrived downtown, parked and started heading toward the building in which the graduation ceremony was being held. We waited in the lobby for a few friends and our pastor at that time and his wife all of whom we had invited locally and showed up. My Pastor's wife must have discerned that there was something weighing on me. She greeted me and then pulled me to the side to ask what was going on. At first, I just told her that it was my family that were up to their same shenanigans of not supporting us as usual, and something within me said, "No, tell her the rest!"

I obeyed and did so. I told her everything from how the morning started with my eye moving involuntarily to the double vision, to the doctor not taking me seriously, to the MRIs, to the technician asking me not just once but thrice did I have a follow-up appointment scheduled, to the phone call I had received on my way to the graduation asking me if I could come in now.

She said, "I'm sure there's nothing serious going on. You know how that ole devil works, always trying to put fear into someone, but..."

I finished the verse for her, "God has not given us a spirit of fear but a spirit of love, power and a sound mind." She said, "That's right, you already know."

Lord knows that my heart was wanting to receive that, but flesh was telling my "sound mind" that something was really wrong. Nonetheless, the auditorium doors opened, and we rushed in to get good seats.

I sat through the entire graduation so proud of my son and trying so hard to enjoy the moment but still wondering what the rush and concern was all about!

After the graduation, we all went out to eat. It was pretty much tradition that I would always feed you if you came to our home or if you came out to an event to support me or my family, and with graduations usually being held on weekdays around here, it had somewhat become tradition that we would meet at a certain restaurant after graduation. My husband and I would pick up the tab for everyone. Thus, tradition continued on that night.

When we got home that night, my husband and I got dressed for bed, and I finally couldn't hold it in any longer. I repeated the same thing to him as I had to our pastor's wife. He also told me not to worry, and he would meet me at the doctor's office tomorrow. He pretended not to be too concerned or worried. That was what he and I did for each other.

All the times he was deployed whether it be combat, peacekeeping, or training missions, our worlds could have been caving in, but one would not tell the other. It was out of respect and pure love for the other. After all, what else could we possibly do for each other when we were in those situations that we weren't already doing? His letters and occasional phone calls (and I do mean occasional) when he was in those very frequent situations (and I do mean frequent) would only state that he was safe and in an undisclosed location and would go on to express his undying love for me and then later, for me and the kids over the years that he continued to serve our Country and God added to our family.

The same thing went for me when I had the chance to communicate with him. I knew he had to be extra focused, and I didn't want him to be worried about something he couldn't control halfway around the world and have the enemy sneak upon him like it was getting ready to do to me the next morning. We kissed goodnight and told each other that we love each other as we always did, mad, sad or not. Like I said, he pretended to not be too concerned, but I knew. Oh yeah, I knew. He even held me a little tighter than usual that night as we both fell asleep.

Chapter 5

I got up and went through my morning routine, no issue with the eye this morning. My husband and I kissed each other and said our I love yous as we always did upon separating and said we would see each other at the doctor's office at lunchtime.

We arrived at the doctor's office about five minutes apart. I waited for him in the parking lot, and we walked in together. I checked in at the front desk, and it just felt like all eyes were on me. Like everyone was in on this big surprise (and not the good kind) except for me. We sat down in the waiting area and waited for my name to be abused again. About ten minutes later, a technician came out and did just that, mispronounced my name. I laughed (not knowing that would be the only laugh I would have for a while) and continued along the hallway. This time, we were led to a consultation room; as we entered, I began to feel a bit uneasy and started praying silently.

The room had a desk with a chair behind it and then a table with a few chairs around the table. My husband and I sat down at the table, and the technician advised us that they would be with us in a moment. Immediately, my thoughts went into overdrive? Who are they? What's going on? What's wrong? Why are we in this room?

What seemed like an eternity suddenly came to an abrupt close when my thoughts were interrupted by the presence of the doctor and a female in business attire who had entered the room. Introductions were made, and then I suddenly witnessed the very condescending doctor from the day before metamorphosing into someone I didn't recognize.

The doctor dimmed the lights and put my skull images on display to explain the situation as he spoke, however, he took the very long way around the diagnosis as I will with you. Bear with me, I just want to paint the perfect picture and make sure I get every word, movement, and gesture absolutely correct. By this time, I had figured out something was definitely wrong, and the lady in plain clothes was a grief counselor.

The doctor pointed to scans and referenced an area at the base of my skull. To me, I had no idea what I was looking at. I recognized the skull but not the dark figure on the slide that appeared to have tentacles stemming from it!

On went the lights, and the doctor began to walk around the office. Here was the entire spill: "I want to apologize for not taking you seriously yesterday. You remind me of a story my grandfather told me that if you'll just listen to people, they will tell you what's wrong with them." His voice was so consoling and caring. I almost wanted to hug him. Then in a flash, he metamorphosed again. Oh yeah, here was the doctor from yesterday!

"Well, I've been doing this for over twenty-two years, and I have only heard of one other case, but it was not in this area and it was nowhere as bad as yours! Anyway, you have an extremely rare brain tumor. That's called Chondrosarcoma of the brain. It's in a very tricky spot, I'm pretty sure it's cancer and no one will be able to help you! In fact, I believe there are only four places in the United States that even fool with them, and only one place in the world for the cancer treatment which is not in this area. But I'll get you in with the top neurosurgeon in this area here to confirm my diagnosis. I'm very sorry. Any questions?"

I promise you that was his delivery of his findings to me verbatim! He had already written me off!

Instead of fear or sadness, I felt a boldness rise up in me and my response to him verbatim was, "This sickness is ***not unto death!***" "When he heard this, Jesus said, '***This sickness will not end in death. No, it is for God's glory so that God's Son may be glorified through it***" (John 11:4).

His face went blank, and I actually felt sorry for him. I discerned he was not a believer, and I refused to let him speak death over me!

"The tongue has the power of life and death, and those who love it will eat its fruit"(Proverbs 18:21).

My husband and I departed his office walking hand in hand. When we got to the parking lot, my husband walked me to my vehicle and embraced me so tight. He wasn't big on public displays of affection, but he held on to me like never before. What in the world? What was happening? I felt moisture on my shoulder, and I practically pushed my husband away from me and looked at him to find him sobbing like I had never seen before in the almost twenty-four years of marriage at that time! He said that he was going back to work to let them know he was taking the rest of the day off. I really just wanted to go back to work, but I felt it best to give in to his wishes since I had never seen him cry like that before. Not when his father died. Not when my mother died. Not even at the news of fallen comrades. Never. He always attempted to hide those types of emotions. He asked me if I was okay, and I told him that I was fine and would see him at home shortly. We kissed and went our separate ways. I couldn't help but think of the irony of the situation.

I had wholeheartedly supported my husband during his nearly twenty-two years of combat service in the United States Army. It had always been him preparing for deployment or war or training, and I was the one crying and clinging to him, and he would be comforting and assuring me everything was going to be fine while keeping the PDA (public display of affection) at hand while in uniform. I knew that whatever his mission was: whether it was invading Panama, guarding the wall at the Czechoslovakian border (before it came down) dividing Germany or storming into one of Saddam Hussein's castles looking for him, that he would be in harm's way and I often feared being a widow. Now the roles had reversed. It was time for me to suit up and prepare for war!

> *"Put on the full armor of God, so that you will be able to stand firm against the schemes of the devil"* (Ephesians 6:11).

I got home a little while before my husband and went upstairs, turned on the television and hubby's crush Robin was wrapping up her morning show. For some reason this prompted the memory of an event that occurred just a few years earlier.

My husband had been unexpectedly deployed (the week following in-processing) to Iraq again and this time was even harder because we (me and the kids) had not yet transferred to the military base in Georgia, so we were still in a non-military community waiting for my husband to get things squared on his end before joining him. That's how we always handled our military reassignments/moves.

Therefore, I did not have that level of support that I was accustomed to when he was deployed in the past and that really made a difference! No one understands your situation quite like someone who is actually going through the same journey.

Nonetheless, I had to remain positive, not show fear in front of the kids and continued to work fulltime. We continued on with our daily routines when my husband was on his final deployment to Iraq but I had become accustomed to watching the news to keep me abreast of things since I had no military chain of support or FSG (Family Support Group) to correspond with, As I would watch the news, I would see the death toll scrolling across the screen and would always pray for the families of those fallen soldiers, but secretly and perhaps selfishly praying that I would not be one of the family members that would get that "dreaded knock at the door" with two Class A uniformed soldiers delivering bad news or offering their condolences.

One night our daughter who was about 8 1/2 came into my room as I was winding down for the evening, I asked her why she was still awake and she said, "Mommy, do you think Daddy is okay or will those bad guys kill him?" I was not prepared for that! I just hugged her real tight and told her that Daddy was going to be fine because God hears our daily prayers that we speak over him. She said she was afraid. I then suggested that she and I say a prayer right then and there for her Daddy and all the troops. After we prayed she said she felt better and was going back to sleep. I wanted that inner peace that she had and as I glanced at the news on my tv in the bedroom and noticed the death toll had increased again from a couple hours ago, I literally cried out to God!

I told him that I was doing my best to be strong and hold on to the faith I had in His promises, but to please, PLEASE give me a sign that my husband was alive and well. I sobbed for a while (something that I would never allow myself to do in front of the kids) and proceeded to shower and prepare for bed.

When I got out of the shower, I put on my pajamas, made sure the alarm was set for the next morning and looked in on the kids. As I opened the doors to both of their bedrooms, I saw that they were fast asleep and I checked all the doors downstairs and came back up to my bedroom.

I would always keep the television on at night (it kind of made me feel *so* not alone) and at a glance I noticed that the death toll had yet increased again! It was then that I decided to turn the channel to *"Nick at Nite"*, turned the volume down low and placed the remote on my night table on top of the alarm clock and remembered watching one of the old black and white sitcoms and eventually fell asleep.

A few hours later, I was startled and awakened by the television blasting at what sounded like full volume and I jumped up and first looked for the remote that was still on top of the alarm clock/radio where I had placed it earlier and then I saw that the time on the clock was 3:16! Then I turned the television down and looked around the room in a puzzled manner, as something caught my attention and was about to give me the peace and reassurance that I had cried out to God for hours earlier.

The television was **somehow** back on the news station and as I looked on in amazement, I saw live footage of a very successful military raid/invasion which was capturing live footage of several armed enemy forces being successfully captured and detained as the US secured control of the town. I was drawn in and didn't know why I couldn't just turn the channel and go back to sleep and then it happened. My husband was in charge of a Special Forces unit out of Fort Benning, GA as the reporter was speaking about the live event and stating what unit it was, the camera zoomed in on soldier who looked so much like my husband that I found myself walking across the room towards the television only to see that when the camera zoomed in extremely close, it was indeed my husband! My husband carries two last names and the name tags on the DCUs (Desert Combat Uniforms/Helmets) were not long enough to fully support both last names: There it was, "CollazoRod"! I couldn't believe what I was witnessing. Then I remembered the VCR on top of the TV in which I kept a VHS tape in it for whenever I wanted to record footage of something I thought my husband would find interesting. I pressed record and it reaired a few minutes later but this time with the caption "Minutes Ago" instead of "Live" and I just watched in amazement.

I went out of my room and down the hall and quietly opened my son's bedroom door and he was not only sleeping but snoring as well. I proceeded further down the hall and opened the door to my daughter's bedroom where she was sound asleep! I went through every room of the house and checking all the locks. Everything was just as I left it hours earlier. I came back up to my room and rewound the tape to watch both the live and reaired broadcast to make sure I wasn't dreaming. I wasn't dreaming! When I saw that live broadcast again and saw the time of 3:16 *For God so loved the world that He gave His only begotten Son, that whosoever believeth shall not perish but have everlasting life!* (John 3:16), I just fell to my knees and thanked God for His miracle confirmation!

I showed the kids the tape later that morning when I awoke them for school. They even brought friends over that evening asking to show them…it was an incredible moment that I will never forget! I even got to share it with hubby when he safely returned home months later.

In hindsight, I realize that just when I felt like I was at my breaking point, and doubt was trying to rear its ugly head and get me off track, God heard my request and confirmed that He was with my husband, with our children and with me…our prayers were *not* going unanswered!

Chapter 6

I was back in the present as hubby arrived home. Our son was at work, and our daughter was at school. We decided not to say anything to the kids until we got more information. In fact, we decided not to tell anyone (besides our pastor at that time and his wife in which neither of them never came to a doctors appointment or to the hospital to see me, as they had promised on several occasions) and that especially hurts because I had worked so hard and given so much in time, labor, and funds and had served so diligently during several years) until we got more information. Secretly, I had another reason for wanting to keep this under wraps. I had always been very peculiar about who I tell my business to as well as who I let pray for me or who I would touch and agree with. Again, it went back to the power of the tongue. Not everyone was for you, and I really didn't want or need any negativity around me or any curses spoken over me at that point.

Something that I had learned as I matured: always listen to what people are saying when they are praying over you, and if you don't understand or don't agree, then don't say amen with them. The word tells us that there is power in prayer. One can put one thousand enemies to flight, two can put ten thousand to flight, etc. *"One of you can put a thousand to flight, because the Lord your God fights for you, just as He promised"* (Joshua 23:10). You don't want to be praying against yourself or God's will for yourself! Sometimes peoples' words are not deliberate with evil intent but can still be used by the enemy with that intent.

We spent the rest of the afternoon doing my favorite thing as a married couple (minds out the gutter folks). We cuddled all afternoon. You all had no idea what a miracle that was! That man couldn't stand to remain in bed unless he was sleeping (or okay, minds back in the gutter). That day, he did that for me; it was so amazing!

Early that evening, the phone rang, and I answered. It was the neurosurgeon's office that I had been referred to confirm the "diagnosis." They scheduled me for an appointment two days later. Things were moving very fast! By that time, our daughter was walking in the door from school. Cuddle time was over, and we had to make up an excuse as to why we were both home during the day.

Normally, I wouldn't get home until around 6:00 p.m. and my husband 10:00 p.m. on a good day. We made up something like an appliance needing repair, and Dad came home to make sure it was repaired correctly. My story to the kids was I came home a little early because of a headache. Headaches had been an ongoing problem for me for some time. I was always told that it was my sinuses and welcome to the sinus/allergy capital of the United States when we moved here.

We ordered Chinese food for dinner that night, and my husband and I watched nothing but comedy sitcoms that night. Thursday morning could not come soon enough (the appointment with the top neurosurgeon in our area). On the other hand, I didn't want this day to end. We knew we both had to go to work tomorrow (Wednesday) and put on our game faces and that was just what we did.

I had already been experiencing insomnia for months, and tonight was no exception. Even though I am a woman of faith and the boldness of the Lord had risen up in me to confess life over this situation and not death, what can I say, I was human and very concerned. In hindsight, I don't think it was so much for myself but for the well-being of my husband and children.

Until Thursday arrived, I found it difficult not to let my mind or thoughts wander; but by the grace of God and the prayers of those who didn't even know they were praying for me, time continued on, and Thursday arrived.

Chapter 7

I shut the alarm clock off before it sounded Thursday morning. I had slept very little. I gave my husband, who was just waking up as well, a good morning kiss and headed for the bathroom. I know it might sound silly, but I wanted to look extra nice that day. So I took my time with my hair and makeup. I thought if I looked better, the news from the neurosurgeon would be better.

We arrived at his office about thirty minutes early. When I entered through the doors, there was such a peace. The office staff was very friendly. I told them who I was and signed in. They told me the doctor was expecting me and to just have a seat; there was no need for any paperwork or insurance info. Wow, what a change!

Thirty minutes later, and right on time I might add, my name was pronounced correctly as I was called to come back to see the doctor.

Instead of an examination room, my husband and I were led right to the neurosurgeon's office. I had done my research on him, and supposedly, he was rated the best neurosurgeon in this city. He was a tall older man who seemed so kind. He shook my hand and then my husband's hand.

We sat down, and he asked if we wanted anything such as coffee, water, etc. We told him we were fine. He then said, "Well, I got your scans from the ophthalmologist, and I will confirm the diagnosis. It's an extremely very rare brain tumor called chondrosarcoma. It's actually a bone tumor that is normally found in the long joints of your body such as your femur, and is usually always benign, but very rarely, it forms or travels. (We're not sure yet) to the base of the skull and attaches itself to the brain. I only know of four places in the United States that operate on them, and if it is indeed cancer, there is one location in the United States that was equipped for the cancer treatment." He said that he had only seen three in his twenty-five years of practice, and mine seemed to be somewhat different from those.

I asked him what he meant by that, and he pointed to the tentacle-like objects on the scan and noted the odd position of my tumor. My husband asked what he meant by rare.

He said it had been close to twelve years since he had seen one, but at that time, he believed the chance of developing one of those were less than a fraction of 1 percent of all the people in the world!

I asked him to repeat that; that figure just couldn't be right! That is just too rare! Today I know it's even more rare than originally thought! It actually happens to *less than 1/16th of 1% of people in the entire world!*

Nonetheless, he gave my husband and me some information on the tumor and on all four locations that treated them. He asked us if we had any questions.

My husband asked him, "What are the odds of survival of this type of tumor?"

The neurosurgeon replied, 'That is something one of the four locations would know more about than myself."

My husband then asked him, "Do you know if it's cancerous?"

He replied, "Once again, that is something that one of the locations will have to answer for you, and imagine that they will conduct a biopsy to confirm."

I asked him what his personal opinion was by looking at the tumor on the scan.

He replied, "If I had to make a guess, I would say, yes, it's cancer. Yes, it's not in the best of locations, but can you beat this? I've seen stranger things occur!" He gave me a hug, shook my husband's hand, and wished us well. He told us to let him know how everything would turn out, and if we needed anything else, to please let him know. We thanked him for his time and left.

When we got to the car, my hubby asked if I wanted to go to breakfast so we could discuss the next move. I told him that I would rather just go back to work and make copies of the information that the doctor had given us, and we could research each place and with it being Thursday, probably decide next week which one to set up an appointment with. He said that sounded like a plan. I dropped him at the house to pick up his vehicle, and we went our separate ways for the day but knowing that our minds would be on the same thing.

When he got home that evening, I gave my hubby his copy of all the reading materials the doctor had given us earlier so that he could read it on his own, and then we could have our "meeting of the minds." I knew he would eventually leave the decision up to me though.

The next few days, we tried to stick to our normal routine so that neither co workers nor our kids would become suspicious. That Sunday, I went to the altar for prayer. I asked for healing, but I also asked that the Lord would direct my path and order my footsteps in making this decision.

Proverbs 3:5-6 says, "***Trust in the Lord with all thine heart, and lean not unto thine own understanding. In all thy ways acknowledge Him and He shall direct your paths.***"

Secondly, we must be in daily prayer. In Jeremiah 33:3, the Lord says, "***Call unto me, and I will answer thee and show you great and mighty things, which you do not know.***"

Thirdly, ***if we want our steps ordered by the Lord, we must believe He will.*** Psalm 37:23.

That night, as I tried to sleep, I could literally hear what sounded like a heartbeat in my right ear. I recalled hearing this on several occasions over the past months but had just brushed it off as previous doctors had when I spoke of that to them. Soon I would learn that was indeed a warning sign.

I must have drifted off to sleep for a while because the sound of the alarm clock startled me. I went down the hallway and made sure that my daughter was up and getting ready for school, and then I went back to my bedroom to pick out something to wear to work and headed to our master bath to shower. My husband was still asleep because his workday started a couple hours later than mine and usually went a lot longer than mine.

When I got out of the shower, my husband was already awake and at the sink brushing his teeth. After he finished, he gave me a hug and kiss. I didn't even ask why he was up early. I knew the answer. I set up glamour camp (makeup, moisturizer, curling iron, etc.) on the vanity, and he then got in the shower.

When he got out of the shower, he told me how beautiful I was. This was something that he did everyday no matter what! He asked me if I had made a choice yet, and I said not really just to see what he would say. I asked him, and he replied the same. I knew it! He was going to leave this up to me. I was a little upset. Don't get me wrong, he was a great husband and father and a much-decorated war hero. Since he was deployed so much, he had always left the budget and household decisions up to me. This time, I just wanted him to treat me like his troops and belt out the orders and lead me into victory! Nothing doing though.

In hindsight, I understood that was a huge decision to make for someone, but give me some input at least! Then it happened! It was like he heard my soul, my thoughts! He said "I was kind of thinking of starting with these two locations" and showed me the info and information he had highlighted. Plus, they were both pretty close to home in comparison to the other two. I was floored because that was my thought process as well. I continued to get ready for work but now actually feeling much lighter on my feet and not so weighed down.

As I got ready to leave for my work commute and drop our daughter off at school on the way, I told him that I would call and set up an appointment on my break today, and then we could see who could see us first. We agreed that was a good starting point, and he kissed me and then pretended to get back in bed and snore as if to rub it in my face that he could do so if he chose to. I made sure I turned the television on *headline news* so he could see one of his celebrity cheats: Robin Meade. I told him to tell Robin to tell Ryan Smith (a correspondent on her morning show) that I said "heeeeeeeyyyy!"

We were goofy that way. I prided myself on always being faithful to him and believing the same for him towards me. I made up this little "celebrity cheat" game. Of course, mine would change more than his. His were usually Robin Meade, Salma Hayek, and Vanessa Williams. Mine were usually Dwayne "the Rock" Johnson, Matthew McConaugheeeeeey, and Frankie G from t*he "Italian Job."* Over the years, I would trade one for Jason Statham and another for Idris Elba now one of them has been replaced with Phil Willis (*Bar Rescue*). The Rock always remained on the list though. Today's list would be Jason Statham, Phil Wills and The Rock (Dwayne Johnson).

Just a couple years earlier, my husband had taken me to WWF Raw being held in our city. The Rock had just come out with his book, and I was determined to get him to sign it. We were waiting/perched around for an hour after the show, and finally, my husband said, "Baby, it's late, and we both have to work tomorrow." Reluctantly, I left my perch and got into the car. We were driving down a six-lane road, three lanes going east and three going west, with a huge meridian in the middle. I looked over and caught a glimpse of "The Rock" and "The Big Show" coming out the side entrance of the building about to enter a limousine. I don't know what came over me, but we were in the outside lane of traffic headed the opposite direction. I grabbed the book, undid my seatbelt, and jumped out of the car and went across six lanes of traffic like *"Frogger"* to get to "The Rock". He was so nice as he signed his book for me and let me act a complete fool around him and thanked me for being such an awesome fan.

In the meantime, I snapped back to reality only to witness my poor husband getting blown at and flipped off as he struggled to drive our manual transmission car, shift gears, and close my door that I had left open in my "groupie haste."

Oops, I am back now. Where was I? Oh yeah, I dropped our daughter off at school and headed to work.

At lunchtime, I closed my office door and began to make phone calls. Both locations faxed me a release of record authorization form for me to sign so that they could get my scans and see what they were working with.

I signed the forms for both facilities, and one called me back later that afternoon to set up a consultation appointment. I scheduled it for the following week in order for my husband and me to each give our jobs notice of needing to take the day off. I knew soon enough we were going to have to talk to at least our immediate supervisors about this missed work time if that were to continue. They said that they would fax me some information to fill out and bring that with me to the appointment along with my insurance information.

Chapter 8

Insurance! I had not even thought that far. How much travel would be involved in this process? Would my insurance cover the procedure(s)? If so, how much? If not, then what would I do?

We had always depended on my income to sustain our household needs and a few perks. I had read through a lot of the material that the neurosurgeon had given us, and treatments and research showed that prices varied greatly!

I thought to myself, *Lord, don't take my health and what little wealth we have too!* After all, our son had incurred college expenses, and our daughter was in her junior year in high school.

Everyone knows how expensive senior year was for a girl: prom, senior pies, memory books, yearbooks, car, and on and on and on; plus college for her would be coming up.

I picked up the phone and called our insurance, which of course was TRICARE due to my husband's retired military status. After being transferred to four different representatives and on hold for what seemed to be an eternity, I was finally transferred to the correct department. I was then informed that it was TRICARE's policy that any travel expenses incurred to see a specialist out of the area/network would have to be paid by the beneficiary first, and then paperwork and receipts would have to be submitted for reimbursement. This included airfare, hotel, gas, rental cars, food, etc.!

Oh boy, this could get very costly quickly. Doctors' fees and tests would require prior authorizations to be paid or reimbursed by them. This was something else to be concerned about: we didn't live beyond our means, but we were by no means rich either. We were blessed enough to pay our tithes and bills, take an annual family vacation, and since we never had a wedding or honeymoon, my husband and I had just started taking an annual cruise. We could float a couple checks but nothing too outrageous!

All four locations were out of town, and I had no idea how many visits would be required or what lay ahead. I decided not to bother my husband at work with this information or concerns. I handled the finances, and there was no need for both of us to be concerned. "***Trust in the Lord and lean not to thou own understanding***" (Proverbs 3:5) was what I kept telling myself.

Well, time to concentrate on work again. I had been working on contracts and data entry while I was on hold with insurance because I ran a little over my lunch hour, but the type of work I did does not allow for errors, so I thought it best to run through it once again. I was an auditor of government/commercial contracts, something like a forensic accountant. I had to take a contract from the proposal and inception phase and monitor it closely and accurately to make sure it was billed to the exact penny, and all agreements were upheld. My head was starting to hurt, and I needed more light.

People would joke and say that my office looked like a living room because I had seasonal throw pillows in the two extra chairs (found in office storage and recovered myself), nice pictures on the walls, a valance on the huge window overlooking the pond/fountain, a stylish floor lamp, and two decorative desk lamps. Sure I loved to decorate (especially for each season/holidays), but I had come to depend on the lamps rather than the standard office overhead fluorescent lighting that had been giving me awful headaches for quite some time (I would learn later that was another symptom to be greatly concerned about).

Chapter 9

Well, twas the night before we traveled to meet with the specialist, so we filled up the tank with gas. Our appointment was early in the morning so we knew we had to leave our house about 5:00 a.m., and the pumps at Sams or Costco would not be open that early. (We would later discover that this was a mistake.) Tricare insisted that your fuel receipts matched the date of our appointment. In other words they didn't care that we were gassing up the night (a few hours before we had to leave before daylight in an effort to save some money and later Tricare denied our travel claim for that petty reason and what they didn't deny took months and months and some additional assistance and action for my husband and I to receive it.

I was sure at this point that the kids were becoming suspicious. My husband and I had been on completely different work schedules and now leaving so early in the morning and together. I told them that we were going to check on their grandfather who had been in and out of the same hospital for some time with various ailments. I hated to lie to them, but again, we just wanted more information before dragging them into the picture and causing them concern.

Our son said he would make sure Jessica was up for school as he left for work. I told Jessica that I would still give her a wake-up call as well from the road.

I gave my little Chihuahua, Zoe (who for some reason had been sleeping on my pillow near my head instead of under the covers at the foot of our bed as she had done since a pup) a kiss and told her to be good.

So we loaded up the Durango with snacks, pillows, and blankets. I loved to fold the second-row seating down and then move to the third-row seating after a while and stretch out. My husband always insisted on driving even when we went on vacation each year. I usually stayed awake to make sure he was alert, but for the past couple long-distance trips, I found myself unable to do so, mainly because of the insomnia I had been incurring for months (hmmm).

My husband told me to go ahead and get comfortable and let him know if I needed him to stop.

God, I love that man! So off we went. About an hour into the drive, my husband asked if I wanted breakfast, and I said, "No." He said, "I'm stopping at McDonald's or somewhere anyhow."

He always did and still insists to this day that I eat breakfast. Even now, he brings me breakfast in bed every morning before he goes to work. Did I mention that I love that man?

So we stopped and picked up something quick. He made me a makeshift table with the cooler in the back, gave me a kiss, and off we went. I called our daughter to make sure she was up for school and reminded her to lock up the house when she left.

About forty-five minutes later, we approached an exit for a rest stop. He asked me if I needed to stretch or use the restroom. I told him that I was good. I had a phobia of public restrooms, and I tried to avoid them at all costs! He took the exit anyway. He got out, came around the vehicle and opened the door on my side since I was in the third-row seating. He asked me to please get out and stretch my legs with him.

As far as rest stops went, it was actually kind of cute. It had an area to go inside as a visitor and sit by the fireplace in rocking chairs. There were brochures everywhere about nearby attractions, and I guess we timed it perfectly. The cleaning crew was just exiting the bathrooms. I could smell the cleaners. My husband waited outside the ladies area as I went, and then I waited for him in the lobby while he went. The attendant at the visitor center was quite nice and even offered us coffee and asked where we were from and where we were going and she wished us good luck and safe travels. My husband said, "We better get back on the road." We got into the vehicle, and as we drove off, something in my spirit told me that this would not be the last time I come here. (Boy, was I right!)

My husband awakened me when we were about fifteen minutes out. He knew I liked to freshen up. You know, fix the bed head and apply my makeup.

After laughing at one of the traffic attendants who was practically dancing as he directed hospital traffic, we pulled into one of the many parking garages at this huge hospital and began to search for a parking space.

We finally found parking and then we exited the vehicle with all the paperwork and directions and proceeded to make our way inside. This place was massive, and it seemed like everyone knew exactly where they were going and just humming around like worker bees.

Even though we had lived and traveled all over the world mostly thanks to Uncle Sam, I still felt like a "Hillbilly in New York City".

We found our way to the neurosurgeon clinic and signed in. Of course, I submitted my paperwork, ID, and insurance info. The staff was very pleasant. I was told to have a seat, and I would be called back shortly.

A few minutes later, I was called back to another waiting area where all my information was again verified and seated in another waiting area. About twenty minutes later, a nurse came and introduced herself and escorted us back to an examination room. Both of my names had been butchered each time.

There was a television in the waiting area and in the examination room, but it was flashing pictures and credentials of all the staff. I couldn't help but notice that one neurosurgeon took up three or four screens. "Impressive," both me and my husband said in sync.

A few minutes later, who walked into the examination room? "Mr. Three or Four Screens" himself! He introduced himself and said that he was the Director of Neurosurgery and that he had reviewed my scans and would personally love to take on my case and was there to answer any questions we might have. We felt pretty honored to have the actual Director of Neurosurgery wanting to personally take on my case; so we started with the following questions and answers:

- What causes them?

   "If I had the answer to that, I could add the Nobel Peace Prize to my accomplishments."

- How rare are they?

   "So rare we really can't even put a percentage on them…my best guess would be somewhere around less than 1/8 of one percent of people in the world! Actually, your chances of winning the lottery, perhaps even twice, are far greater than ever getting one of these." (We now know it happens to less the 1/16 of 1% of people in the world)

- Can I trade?

   He laughed. "I know right!"

- So how many of these particular procedures do you perform a year?

  "Good question! As I mentioned before, they are pretty rare, but now I am actually traveling as my schedule allows about a month out of every year to conduct or oversee this procedure in other countries/continents…so maybe three or four."

- What is the success rate with this type of tumor both cancerous and noncancerous?

  "Another great question. I personally have never seen or heard of a recurrence after successful retraction and/or cancer treatment if deemed necessary."

It is now that I realize that I had failed to ask him about life expectancy. I have since learned that the expectancy is about two years on average and beyond five years was unheard of. I am now over fifteen years out! Glory! Readers, are you thinking what I'm thinking? Perhaps God did not have me ask that question at that time because it could have further frightened me or made me back out altogether! ***Mind blown! Some 15 years later and I am still seeing God's Hands in it all!***

- What is the average recovery time for such a procedure?

  "Wow, you are locked and loaded with the questions. There are several variants that will affect this

such as if it is cancerous, if so, what stage, the age and health of the individual to begin with, what all has to be done to extract the tumor, and of course, aftercare-the most likely being you are susceptible to infection or other complications."

- What do you mean by what has to be done to extract the tumor?

   "Glad you asked that, I have asked a colleague of mine to join us. He often assists me with this type of procedure. He is an otolaryngologist and deals with things such as rerouting of the nerves and sinus com-plications and other delicate matters if needed, and if you choose to have your procedure done here, he will also assist with the performance of the biopsy of the tumor to determine if it is cancerous or not. He and I have collaborated on several of these procedures and others. He is very well respected in his field!"

A few moments later, there was a knock at the door. The door opened and in walked an older gentleman in dress slacks and a white doctor's coat with a younger woman in civilian clothes. They introduced themselves as the otolar-yngologist and "skull-base tumor coordinator".

The neurosurgeon went on to say that this was the col-league that he was speaking of, and the young lady would serve as a liaison between all of us in coordinating appoint-ments, tests, surgery, etc. since there would be times that

I might not have to see both on the same visit. The neurosurgeon did make it clear that if chosen, he would be in charge of my case, and all decisions would go through him.

The otolaryngologist asked if I had any questions for him. My questions and his responses were the following:

- I understand that you would be assisting the neurosurgeon with this procedure?

  "Indeed, he and I have worked together successfully many times before and would welcome the opportunity to take care of you, young lady."
- You had me at "young lady"! *(Laughing)* Speaking of which, does this tumor have a preference in victims i.e., sex, age, occupation, ethnicity, etc.?

  "No, so far, we have not been able to find a common link reviewing your scans, though I suspect yours has been there for a while and has just started causing you noticeable trouble." (I would later learn why he said that and wonder why I didn't think to ask him at that time.)

He then said if we had any further questions or concerns that we could call the skull-base tumor liaison he had introduced us to. She was very pleasant but seemed a little unorganized. She apologized for this and also informed my husband and me that she was new to the position but would work her hardest to keep the doors of communication open between myself and the two surgeons. She apologized for not yet having business cards but did write her name and information down on a sheet of notebook paper from a spiral notebook that she had been making notes in and tore it off and gave it to me. I remembered saying to my husband sarcastically, "Now that's professional!"

Hubby said, "Give her a break, she says she is new to the position but will work hard for us."

This was a turn of events. Even though both my husband and I are Geminis as well as "neat freaks", he hated disorganization the most! I thought that would have been an immediate turnoff or 'bout face for us to not proceed with this facility and go visit the next one. I would chalk that up to twenty-two years of combat military service in the United States Army! HUA! Instead, he surprised me by coming to her defense. (I would find out later that this was all part of God's plan: this position was recently created for her and I was where I was supposed to be. God had answered the righteous prayers and seemed to have strategically hand-picked every professional that was about to embark on this miraculous journey with me.) She was a wonderful person and "this sickness was **Not unto Death**"!

Well, we got everyone's contact information, shook hands, and even got a small tour around the huge facility. As we got ready to depart, the neurosurgeon stated, "Please take your time and research the other facilities. They too are qualified as well. I just wouldn't take too much time in case the tumor is indeed cancerous."

The otolaryngologist then stated that if we decided to go with them, the next appointment would be to discuss performing a biopsy of the tumor that he would perform to test for cancer and if so, what stage. Both doctors would be directly involved with this procedure. Together they would decide the approach they thought best to get a sample of the tumor.

We all thanked one another for our time and shook hands again. I of course, being a hugger, had to give all involved a hug and tell them that, "We would be praying on it!"

The skull-base tumor liaison walked us to the front door of the clinic. She was very friendly and said we could call or page her day or night with any questions we might think of, and she would get the answers for us promptly!

My husband asked me how I felt about the meeting, and I said that I was very impressed with their credentials and that they seemed to have a very caring spirit as well. We headed to the parking garage to find our car and grab something to eat as we headed back home.

We stopped at an O'Charley's restaurant that was really not the norm for us, but everyone was quite pleasant, and we did enjoy the food. As usual, I couldn't finish mine, so I packed it up to go. I knew I would nibble on it on the journey back. We each just ordered a lunch special and a drink.

I reminded my husband to keep the receipt for reimbursement. (Little did I know then that this would become a very familiar routine for us, and we would have to battle for all reimbursements down the road, and I do mean battle!) A little further down the road, we discovered some shopping outlets. At that time, I was still bringing home a really good income; and with my husband's income, we were on top of things. We looked at a few stores and purchased, I think, two items. One was for me from the Nike outlet! (I was surprised too. I thought the price sign had fallen down in shock as I passed by it.) Anyway, I bought the very last pair that happened to be my size of a moccasin type shoe on the clearance rack (this girl loves a sale) that had the Nike support and tread underneath, and they were amazingly different and comfortable! They were standing alone on the clearance shelf categorized under the wrong size but just staring at me! I searched the entire store to see if they had others, and they didn't. It gets better, when we went to the front to pay for them, they rang up half price plus they gave us a military discount of either 10 or 20 percent! (Little did I know that God was going to continue to perform blessings for us throughout this journey.) To this day some 15 years later, I still get compliments on those shoes, and everyone wants to know where I got them. I've looked for them several times through several resources over the years to no avail. If I ever find them again I will purchase several more! My husband grabbed his item and got his military discount, and we were back on the interstate.

We talked for a while as I periodically. nibbled and slept on the journey back home. We finally arrived home that evening. We had leftover lasagna and salad from yesterday's dinner that I had prepared after work, so thank You, Lord, I didn't have to cook. I showered and got into my pajamas.

Our son was en route to see a friend, and our daughter was in her room on her man-made body extension from her ear (cell phone). I gave her a hug. She was not much of a hugger, but I did it anyway. I asked if she had a good day at school, finished homework, was hungry…you know, the usual. She said she was fine, and her day was fine. I could tell that she sensed something was going on, but she just remained silent for a minute and said, "Okay, Mom, I'm on the phone…I'll come see you later!"

I thought it was then that I made the decision of where to have my brain surgery. We had just ridden almost a five hundred mile round trip, and I really couldn't see myself going all across the country for months going through this same process: taking off work, keeping secrets, and wondering if it was cancerous after all, if it was, wouldn't it be advancing somewhat every day?

I had never been a "buy at your first stop" kind of girl, but I would really need to pray on this. My husband and I were very impressed with the consultation and their reputation and credentials. "Oh, Lord, I prayed, give me confirmation!"

We kissed each other good night, and for the first time in quite some time, I got about five consecutive hours of sleep even though Zoe was once again sleeping on my pillow near my head instead of under the covers at the foot of the bed as she had done since we got her eleven years earlier. This was something she started doing probably close to a year prior to me taking notice of some odd things that I now realize were actually asymptomatic. My husband said she was just getting older, and she had always been very protective of me.

In hindsight, I realize that my body had been trying to warn me for years that something wasn't right.

Chapter 10

That next morning, as we both got ready for work, I was in the shower, and my hubby was brushing his teeth. I yelled out to him, "Hey, babe, I've been thinking that maybe I should-" And in unison, we both said the same thing together! There was my confirmation. God was something else!

I asked him why he chose the same facility, and he pretty much said for the same reasons I had. The only thing he disagreed with me was when I said if need be if something went critically wrong, most of my immediate family was forty-five miles away from that facility. He frowned, and though I knew what that meant, I asked him anyway.

He said, "You know good and well we cannot count on those people. They let you sit up here with fourteen fractures after being hit head-on by some ridiculous driver who had been the cause of 4 accidents in 2 years in which *ALL* vehicles were totaled who is somehow still terrorizing people on the roads and didn't come and see you one time during the whole ordeal!" Plus, they never came to visit you and the kids once while I was deployed and I'm just gonna stop there! He was absolutely correct! Especially since two years earlier when my middle sister had been involved in a car wreck, and sustained no fractures but did require surgery on her spleen, I immediately went there and checked on her and brought her two girls back home with me for 12 days and exhausted all of my PTO while keeping them entertained in an effort to keep them from worrying about their Mom and how did she repay me? She picked them up the day before my birthday and not only didn't even give me a card, but I barely got a verbal thank you. She did wish me Happy Birthday.

I knew this was probably the touchiest subject in our marriage. Something told me to proceed with caution, but I didn't, as I belted out, "Your family has never been here for us either!

His family was in Puerto Rico and weren't exactly rich, but we had given his family a lot over the years and some did have the means to do what they wanted. The truth was neither I nor my children had ever been accepted by my husband's family. His mother had never accepted that he did not marry a Puerto Rican and/or Catholic girl, and even though our children carried some of her DNA, it didn't matter. Yet our money was always welcomed when they called or wrote for it!

A few years earlier, my husband's only brother in Puerto Rico had been shot in the stomach, so my husband was granted emergency leave time from the Army. Without hesitation, we scrounged up the money for four round-trip plane tickets with an open-end date for return. Yes, we, including the two kids, were accompanying him and would be staying with one of his family members, who had three young boys. I was told by my husband that everything was worked out because the three boys could go next door and stay with their grandparents, and the four of us would use their room. When we arrived at the airport in San Juan, my husband's brother-in-law picked us up and dropped us off at his home and then he went back to work.

Upon entering, all I wanted to do was get my nine-year-old son and three-and-a-half-year-old daughter situated. There were only two bedrooms in the house, so my husband put the suitcases down, and we saw the three single beds in the room. They were stripped down to the mattresses with no pillows in sight. I wasn't expecting "the Four Seasons," but the basics would be nice. After all, I do believe you get a pillow and a blanket even in prison. I thought about pushing two of the beds together so my husband, daughter, and I could sleep together and put our son on the other single bed, but the angle of the room would not allow for that. So, hubby and I went to look for linens, pillows, towels, washcloths, etc., to no avail. My husband was told there was no need to rent a car or hotel, yet we were without transportation (no Ubers back then) and even the basics.

Now this particular sister and her older husband were given the house by his parents which had enabled them to pay for their brand new Toyota Avalon in full. They both worked and I know that they had the means to provide basic necessities for us and it made me so mad! Even though I knew this, I remained silent for the time.

I always traveled with a pillow and blanket, so I got the kids settled on a bed with the pillow and blanket that I had traveled with. When his family members got home that night, they and my husband began speaking in Spanish. I understood a lot of Spanish but tended to answer back in English. From what I understood, my husband was asking about the no pillows, linen situation and if there were any stores open to purchase the things we needed and was told no. He asked to borrow one of their vehicles the next day to purchase stuff we needed.

They both said they needed their vehicles, but the husband had a shop where they fixed, detailed, painted, etc., vehicles and would find him something. They heated up some food for us, and I fed the kids (I was not about to eat) so that I could get them back in bed. I could tell that my husband was both embarrassed and mad. We had come all that way and were treated like we were filthy creatures not worthy of the bare essentials. Early the next morning, my husband left out walking and found a little bodega in the neighborhood and brought back some towels, cereal, milk, and snacks. We fed the kids, and my husband started making phone calls.

By early afternoon, someone arrived with a little car for us to use. I wasn't sure if it would make it anywhere or not, but we were about to find out. As we were leaving, the grandmother and her daughter, who spoke really good English and lived next door, introduced themselves and asked where we were going. My husband told them we were going to the hospital to see his brother. I intervened and asked for directions to any store where we could buy bedding. They looked confused and entered the house, then went back to the bedrooms and looked. The grandmother shook her head in disbelief and said she was so sorry. She said she didn't understand why there weren't pillows or linens on the bed because she was using her extra linens for the boys that had beds at her house and did not see any in the laundry. The daughter told us how to get to a store to purchase the items we needed.

We found the store. Though costly, we bought bedding for three beds, towels, and washcloths. Then we found a food market, and I bought food to make for everyone, including items to make some favorite Puerto Rican dishes such as arroz con polio (chicken and rice stew). I normally make my own sofrito, which is a seasoning base used in most Puerto Rican dishes and requires several types of produce, herbs and a blender to puree it all, but this time I bought sofrito in the bottles to make dinner. We took everything home, showered and changed, and headed to the hospital to see his brother. When we got to the room, my husband's mother, one of his sisters, and his brother's girlfriend were there.

It was my first time meeting his brother, and my husband introduced me and the kids to him. We stayed for a couple of hours, but the kids were getting bored and fidgety, and hubby told him we would be back to see him. I had met his mother on two occasions only because following my husband's father's premature death, she had been staying in Chicago for a while with one of her sisters. That sister and her husband took her on a road trip, and one of the stops was to see us in Tennessee since I had very recently given birth to our first child. She met my son as an infant, my parents and a few of my siblings. My Dad barbequed and he and my Mom really poured on the hospitality. In fact, my husband was still on leave from me giving birth and we were all staying at my parent's house (before the battered women's shelter incident).

The second time I made her acquaintance was on another road trip with her sister and brother-in-law. They had also brought their son and another one of her sisters and her boys. Both of her sisters were very nice and we made them feel welcomed. We even had them follow us to meet our grandparents (on my mother's side). My grandparents lived on a street that had only one house that we had lived in for five years and there was a beautiful river with boating, fishing and picnic areas. I have had some good communication over the years with them and they adored my husband. It's a shame that I can't say the same for my mother-in-law or the rest of the family; unless there is a financial need. We have been contacted countless times for financial assistance and now some of their kids have even called us for financial help several times over the years. At this time, my husband had returned to Germany to finish out the last few weeks of that tour. Our son had just turned two years old. We all took a trip to the local zoo with the kids. It was amazing to see how much my son looked like his cousins. My son looked purely Puerto Rican at that time, but I guess that wasn't good enough.

Well back to our "nightmare visit to Puerto Rico": we left the hospital, and when we got back to the house, I began preparing arroz con polio for the entire family. That soon came to an end when a couple of his sisters showed up and insisted I was doing it all wrong and were laughing at me. I am a great cook and I knew for a fact I was preparing it correctly; that was just another opportunity for them to take a jab at me and their brother for leaving Puerto Rico in an attempt to live a better life. I had met my husband at the military base (in which he had already been in the Army nearly two years) near my home, The same base that I was born, but according to the way I was treated by his immediate family, one would think that I came to Puerto Rico, singled him out and took him hostage! I became frustrated and left the room. In fact, I left the house and went for a walk around the neighborhood. I ran into the bodega my husband must have found the day before. When I returned to the house, I put the linens on all the beds and then showered and went to bed. It was so hot in the room.

We had the only window in the room open, but it wasn't helping. My husband left the room and came back with a fan. One of those square ones that sat on the floor and blew air in one direction. Eventually, I fell asleep only to be awakened by the neighbor's rooster (every morning) at 4:45 am, and the next day, we went to his mother's house for dinner. To my surprise that evening she was very nice to us, showing me photographs after dinner, but never tried to bond with the kids.

As I write this I can't help but feel pity for anyone who would deny their bloodline based on ethnicity or religion. She and all the others as well as many of my family members missed out on some amazing kids! I know we as parents all feel that way about or kids, but I am reminded of the calling that I truly believe that both of my kids have on their lives and the spiritual gifts they have:

1. When my son was 2 ½, my husband was deployed to Desert Storm and of course we were stationed in Ft Hood, TX and had no family to call upon. I ended up having to have my wisdom teeth cut out and developed a dry socket. Thankfully my son was the only child at this point and was really well behaved. As I suffered in pain for a few days,

he would sit on the floor beside me as I laid on the living room couch and play with his toys for hours or watch television. One time I managed to drift off to sleep and when I awoke, he was rubbing my forehead and praying over me and speaking in tongues!

2. Just as he turned 4, we were stationed in Germany for a second time. My husband was at work and I was working part-time, but had the day off. As I was watching the one American television station, he was once again engrossed with his toys since the kid shows were not yet on for another few hours. I can remember him coming up to me and hopping into my lap about 5 months after we arrived in Germany. He said, "Guess what Mommy…you're going to have me a baby sister and her name is going to be Jessica!" As I looked at him in amazement and shock, he told me exactly what she was going to look like…down to the mark (birthmark) on the side of her forehead. As soon as he told me that, he just jumped down and went back to playing with his toys. I was speechless for a few minutes and then just blew it off. As I recalled that memory later that night when I was in bed, it hit me that I had not had my cycle since we arrived in Germany. This had happened to me on our first tour to Germany and found out four

months later that I was pregnant with him. I still tried to deny the validation of what he said earlier by recalling that doctors had switched my birth control pill on my first doctor's visit at the military infirmary because the pill I had been on was not available there, plus I had also been on antibiotics for tonsillitis weeks earlier, but this was before medical research had revealed or discovered that antibiotics can negate the power of oral contraceptives. I tried to go to sleep but his words just kept replaying in my mind. Well a few weeks later, I decided to go to the infirmary for a pregnancy test. I just knew that once it came back negative, things would calm down and my cycle would regulate. Well guess what? I was a good estimated 7 weeks pregnant. I had ultrasounds during that pregnancy but just like when I had been pregnant with him years earlier, the baby was never in the right position to ascertain the gender, but about 7 months later, I gave birth to a 9Ib baby girl. When she came out and was cleaned up, she was placed on my chest and she looked exactly as he had told me she would right down to the birthmark! Needless to say, I gave her the name Jessica and the middle name of Gabrielle (with the meaning of God is my strength)!

3. Also about 2 months before she was born, my husband was off in Grafenwoehr, Germany or as they called it "The Dust Bowl" on training maneuvers. My son and I had went grocery shopping the day before and we lived on the third floor (with 2 flights of stairs) on each level, so as I unloaded the car, my then 5 year old son would say, "Mommy, remember Daddy said I am the man of the house when he's away so I will carry the heavy stuff up the stairs!" He was always and still is amazingly strong as I recall him carrying gallons of milk or laundry detergent up those 6 flights of stairs. The next morning, we got ready to leave for Church. This vehicle was purchased brand new 2 months prior and had worked fine the day before when we were out running Saturday errands, but as I opened the door and got my son in his booster seat and came back around the vehicle and placed my purse and bible in the front seat, to my surprise the vehicle would not start. My kitchen window overlooked the parking lot where I parked it the night before and nothing was left on. After a couple of tries, I told my son to wait there while I buzzed a neighbor who had a desk job and never deployed or went out for training on the intercom system of the building to see if he could come and take a look at our car. When I got to the car less than a

minute or two later, I told my son that our neighbor was coming down to look at our car and he just said very "matter factly", "Mommy, we don't need that man to help us with our car because I asked Jesus to heal our car and if you turn the key our car is going to start." I actually paused, and just looked at him and he repeated himself. I took the key and placed it in the ignition…vrmmmmmmm off to Church we went!

4. I see those same gifts in my daughter as well. My daughter only knew/met her grandma (my Mom) for a few weeks of her life. We returned from Germany when our daughter was 2 ½ and hesitantly stayed with my parents for 2 weeks before reporting to Ft. Riley KS in May of 1996. We saw my mom again for the last time in August of 1996 when we went to bury her father (my grandpa). Jessica had just turned 3 a few days before that and then a few months later (November 1996) my mother unexpectedly left this world. When me, my husband and kids went to make funeral arrangements for my Mom, we ended up staying at my middle sister's house. Things were calming down from a very stressful and hectic day of planning. I fed and bathed Jessica and she and our son who was 8 ½ at that time, went to bed in one of the bedrooms. A couple hours later all hell broke

out between 2 of my sisters. As I saw that it was about to get physical, I went outside to get my husband, my younger brother and my middle -sister's boyfriend to help deescalate things. As the four of us were entering the house, Jessica came down the hall carrying her favorite stuffed animal and calmly walked between those 2 sisters who were fiercely arguing and very sternly said, "Grandma said stop it! Stop it right now!" She said nothing else as the room became silent and it seemed that someone had hit the pause button. She turned around and went right back to bed. There was peace for the remainder of the night. She is also an excellent judge of character and senses negativity or evil in people that eventually always proves to be correct.

Okay, so back to Puerto Rico, at that time, our daughter (who was extremely fair-skinned and sometimes mistook for Caucasian) was the only granddaughter on my husband's side of the family. There were seven (including ours) grandsons at that time. I remember one of the sisters had three boys: one had blonde hair and blue eyes; the second son had sandy brown hair and blue eyes; and the youngest had red hair and green eyes, I couldn't believe that with all this diversity within this culture, my beautiful children were not accepted by flesh and blood. We were able to see his brother get discharged from the hospital, and he went to his girlfriend's house to recover. It was a beautiful home, and her family was quite nice to us when we came by to visit his brother the day before we were leaving. Needless to say, I, nor my children, never went back to Puerto Rico; however, our money has made numerous one-way trips, and my husband has returned when needed.

This has been an ongoing issue in our marriage. I knew that because of the Army. We had lived all over the world, but since we got back to the US, to our home state nonetheless in 1998, my husband had been deployed several times, I had been hit full frontal head-on and sustained fourteen fractures, I raised my drug addicted sister's oldest son for three years while I was single parenting my two children due to combat deployments, I sent money to loved ones count less times, and when it was time to give back, my husband was right! I had been let down time and time again.

Don't get me wrong. We still had love for one another, but things had changed for some of us and not necessarily for the better. Yet I still had so much love for them, and I guess hope as well. I was the middle of seven children, three brothers and three sisters. Our mother had passed away in 1996 just four months after her father (the world's greatest grandpa), and it seemed that things weren't and never would be the same again. (Who knows? Maybe another day, maybe another book?) I had not seen my mother in four years; she met my daughter for the first time and six months later, she unexpectedly left this world.

Before the situation could escalate, I gave my husband a kiss, and we apologized to each other and embraced. We both came from dysfunctional backgrounds and strived hard not to expose our children to that chaotic lifestyle but instead break the generational curses!

I finished dressing and told hubby that I loved him and told my daughter it was time to go, and we left for our usual routines.

When I got to work, I said my good mornings and pushed my office door up just a bit in an effort for privacy. I knew that the facility was one hour behind my time zone, but if anything, I could leave a message. I dialed the number to the skull-based coordinator and told her that we had decided to proceed with them and to please contact us with the next step.

The morning seemed to fly by as my overflowing inbox took my mind off things for a while. My position had been given a goal each month of how many contracts to audit, and everyone else on my team worked from home and lived in other states. I always pushed myself to exceed those goals; even early on, I was already completing more than some auditors who had been on the job for seventeen years! That too would go unappreciated as well as all my accomplishments at that job.

Out of nowhere, the phone rang and startled me. I saw the area code and knew that it must be coming from the facility we chose.

I answered, and on the other end was the skull-based coordinator. She said she had received my message and was in the process of coordinating everything with my insurance, physicians, and the facilities' OR, and I should expect to hear back from her that week. I thanked her and took a deep breath before I called my husband.

Two days later, I received a call back with the information regarding the approval as well as the date and time of the biopsy. She said she understood that we were traveling a good distance and didn't want to keep missing work at this point, so it was scheduled for a late Friday evening, and barring no complications, I should be released that Saturday because the doctor was considering going with a less invasive approach (why didn't I ask what that approach actually was). I found that to be very considerate and interesting. I only wish now that I knew that the less invasive approach would and still does cause me a lifetime of several restrictions and issues.

She asked me for my fax number so that she could fax me the information we just discussed as well as the approval she received from my insurance and their policy on reimbursement. I was instructed to not eat or drink anything for at least eight hours prior. That was going to be a little difficult. Not because of breakfast or lunch but I so loved to snack at leisure on the drive there.

It still would involve some loss work especially for my husband, but it was manageable. I immediately called my husband, and we both put in for the time off that was in a couple weeks. I remember looking at the calendar and being so happy that it was scheduled for after the NFL draft. Yes, I grew up cheering for the Pittsburgh Steelers since I was four years old. My mom said my dad would sit down to watch the Steelers games; he would have a beer and a cigar, and I would get a crayon and a Shasta. My dad would take a puff of his cigar and I would take a puff of my crayon. My dad would take a sip of his beer and I would take a sip of my Shasta. He would celebrate or cuss and I would reciprocate his actions. It was through this that I eventually came to understand the game to include rules, plays, signals, the difference between a 3-4 and a 4-3 defense, zone and man to man coverage, a nickel package and pretty much everything. Even today many people, especially guys, are often surprised, impressed, or even threatened by my knowledge of both football and the Steelers.

Chapter 11

That Friday in early May finally arrived. Since my husband's birthday was in May, we told the kids that we were taking an overnight trip for Dad's birthday present.

I was so glad that our son was still living at home after graduating college valedictorian, and that our daughter had already planned to be at a sleepover. Their personalities were totally different. My son was a homebody and a "neat freak"! You could go in his room and move an ink pen, and I promise you, he would return home later and ask, "Who's been in my room?" Also, he had turned my dining room into a computer lab and workshop. He was always fixing or building computers from the ground up for people for free! Now my daughter, she was smart as well but more of a social butterfly. She had to be doing something or going somewhere all the time, and her room-Lord, that room! I knew I could have filed FEMA claims and been successful!

So Friday came, and we loaded up the Durango and hit the road this time with suitcases plus the usual snacks (that I couldn't have until afterwards), cooler, pillows, and blanket to make my ride comfortable.

My husband asked if I needed to stop as we approached the cute little rest stop from last trip.

I laughed and said, "It's not like I have anything in my stomach or bladder."

He said, "Oh yeah, but I need to stop and stretch my legs and use the restroom."

I followed him inside and again was greeted by a very friendly staff. They asked where we were headed, and me being the talker that I am but in a good way told them where and why. They wished us luck, and one lady who overheard the conversation said, "I will be praying for you." My husband is always amazed how complete strangers walk up to me and tell me their life stories, but this time, I was that stranger. I told them, but besides them, only my hubby, pastor (at that time), his wife, and doctors knew. I still chose to keep it that way until that moment with the strangers...hmmm. I truly believe God's angels are dispatched all over the world and strategically placed in our path when we are in need!

We arrived at the hospital, and we were instructed to park somewhere completely different this time. We got inside and asked the front desk to page the skull-base tumor coordinator, once again my name was mispronounced as we were leaving. I could hear the same lady calling the name "Jesus Gonzalez" (but pronouncing it like *Jesus in the Bible*). She called for Jesus three (3) times, each time louder and louder before my humor (coping mechanism) kicked in and I stopped and my husband took a few steps and realized that I wasn't next to him and he turned around and asked me what I was doing and I told him, "I'm waiting on *Jesus* to show up. If **He** shows up, then **He** can fix all of this for me right now." He laughed and came and grabbed my hand to lead me to the next destination of the hospital. And a few minutes later, we were met by the skull-base coordinator and directed to a different part of the hospital.

We arrived in a room to find both doctors waiting on us. They shook my husband's hand, and I, of course, gave out hugs. The otolaryngologist explained that he was contemplating a less invasive approach for the biopsy. He really didn't want to saw my skull open at this point unless that approach didn't work. In hindsight, I should have asked more questions about this "less invasive" approach, but there was no way to see the problems that would result from that even to this day. So I probably would have kept things as they were. After all, anything sounded better than having your skull sawed open.

After a brief conversation, we were escorted to the surgical waiting area. I began to get a little anxious. I told my husband that maybe he should go ahead and get my bag and stuff from the vehicle. He told me to relax and that once they had a room for me, he would grab everything and make sure I was good to go.

A few minutes later, my name was called, and my husband was told to wait there for me. They were just going to get me in a gown and get my vitals, and then they would call him back, and that was just what they did.

As my husband and I were waiting, I looked at him holding my personal belongings in two hospital bags (yes, I was extra sometimes), and I began to tear up. I thought of the worst and how he would carry on without me and the kids etc. He said, "Don't even try it! Everything is going to be fine, girl!"

He was giving me a big kiss as the anesthesiologist flipped the curtain and walked in to introduce himself. He went through all the usual questions and explained his role and the risks of anesthesia and asked me if I had any questions. Afterwards, I signed the consent form, and he laughed and said, "As you were." I blushed because I knew my hubby was embarrassed too.

A few minutes later, they came for me, and my husband was told where to wait, and he told me he loved me, and he would see me soon. I began to pray silently. I remembered the doors opening to the OR. It was smaller than I thought it would be, but I guess my expectancy was magnified because we were talking about the brain here. (Please keep that statement in mind for future reference.)

I remembered everything to be really bright, the mask going over my face, the smell of clean air, and counting backward from one hundred. The last number I remembered was eighty six (as in Hines Ward-Pittsburgh Steelers).

Chapter 12

When I awakened, I was in a room. I opened my eyes, and a nurse was asking me my name, and did I know what day it was and what year it was? I felt extremely rested yet extremely nauseated. I answered the questions, but I felt so sick to my stomach! The nurse said she was going to get the doctor and would be right back! Moments later, the otolaryngologist entered the room; and by this time, my husband was at my side. The doctor said, "I understand that you are feeling nauseated" and I replied, "Yes!" He then stated, "that is more than likely a side effect of the anesthesia. We'll start some Phenergan or Zofran in your IV to get you some relief." (The nurse left to get some as he continued to talk.) "You did great. To make a long story short, I went up through your right nostril, burst through both sinus cavities, and went to the back of your brain and took out some samples of the tumor to send off." I really couldn't process what he was saying nor did I know that this less invasive procedure would permanently and invasively impact my life forever because I was having the dry heaves so bad!

The nausea and dry heaves continued on through the night, all day Saturday, and into early Sunday morning. The worst kind of nausea where you couldn't eat or throw up, but you had the urge to do both! My husband never left my side. He slept in the uncomfortable recliner in the room and showered in my room and would go down to the cafeteria and eat there because I couldn't stand to smell the food. (God, I love that man. I may have mentioned that before.) Finally, when the doctor made his rounds on Sunday afternoon, he saw that I was able to keep the liquid diet down and toast plus the nausea had subsided. He said that he would notate in my records not to use that particular "cocktail" for anesthesia next time (what next time was he referring to? He must have known something but just left it at that.) My vitals were good, and even though I felt a little weak, I was ready to get out of there! He signed my discharge papers that included all at home instructions.

Hubby packed up all my things, and we hit the road. Next thing you know, we refueled the vehicle and found ourselves at the same O'Charley's again. We even had the same server as before, and she sat us in the same booth as last time. I remembered ordering their loaded potato soup even though it was May and eating their delicious rolls and praying that the nausea would not return. Hubby reminded me to go slow. I managed to eat two rolls and most of the soup and drink two glasses of sweet tea. The server wrapped up some of everything to go as well. She was awesome. We got to the vehicle and put the meal receipts in with gas receipts we had been collecting in an envelope in the glove compartment, that we always kept there before photocopying them and submitting them to our insurance for reimbursement and off we went.

About halfway into the drive, we approached our little rest stop; and before my husband could ask, I said, "Yes." We got out and went inside. I recognized one person on duty; they were in the middle of a shift change. I left word with the one I knew to tell the others that everything went fine, and I would see them next trip. Looking back, I guess my spirit sensed something was wrong.

Chapter 13

A couple weeks went by, and I did my best to keep my mind off the pending test results.

Before I knew it, June eighteenth (my forty-fourth birthday) had arrived. As I awoke and thanked God for another day and birthday, my husband and daughter entered the bedroom with a card and two flower arrangements. Our son had already left for work but had placed some money in the card for me. They even remembered that tulips were my favorite flower with yellow roses in a close second place. I began to cry as I read the cards. This year, I could tell that they put a lot of effort in picking out a card that just seemed perfect.

I hugged and kissed them both and realized I better get a move on if I wanted to miss the horrible traffic that occurs after a certain time in the morning on my commute to work.

I could remember my husband saying, "Don't forget to think about where you would like to go for dinner tonight!" I smiled and headed for the bathroom. I normally tried to take my birthday off because our company considered employees' birthdays a holiday and this year my birthday fell on a Friday. Of course, not knowing how much time I would need to take off in the future if surgery/recovery was necessary, I decided to work and use the day at a later time. Anyhow, I would only be home wondering about the test results; at least work would take my mind off things for a while anyhow. I finished getting ready and grabbed both flower arrangements and a vase so I could make a combined arrangement of both flowers together to put on my desk. I got to work a few minutes early and started to work on my flower arrangement.

A few minutes later, a couple of my coworkers passed by my office and invited me to lunch for my birthday. They were like, Wasabi today? That was always a special treat for us. We worked in a very small town in Oak Ridge, Tennessee, and our restaurant options were quite limited. We relished the rare occasions in which we could work through our breaks and go on our sixty mile round trip commute into Knoxville for something not offered where we worked. Though I could never come close to finishing even the lunch portions, the show that the chef would put on and just a little extra time away from the office made it worthwhile.

That night, my husband planned to continue the birthday celebration by taking me out to dinner at our favorite Mexican restaurant with our neighbor friends who lived across the street at the time.

That evening as I was getting ready for what I was hoping would be a fun and distracting occasion, the phone rang, and it was the skull-base tumor coordinator. She asked how I was doing, and I told her fine under the circumstances. She then proceeded to tell me that the results had come back from the biopsy, and they were positive for cancer. I paused for a moment as I felt my heart drop, and I could remember her asking me if I was okay. I told her, "Yes, and thank you for the birthday present." She said, "Today is your birthday?" I replied, "Yes."

She apologized. She claimed she didn't look at my date of birth in my records but did want to let me know that the surgery was scheduled for July 27, 2010. She said she would be in touch with more details regarding the surgery, and I sarcastically thanked her yet again. Happy freaking birthday to me! I hung up the phone and went to the bathroom to tell my husband. He looked shocked for a minute, and then he came and held me really tight and said that all would be okay. We would just enjoy tonight, and we could talk about it tomorrow or later. He didn't want to mess up my birthday. Too late! I decided then that the woman who was forty-four years old today and had only been drunk twice in her whole life that tonight was going to be number three! I guess I let the shock of the news steal my joy and thought it was going to be my last birthday. So I was going to make it memorable.

I felt betrayed by God. All the prayers and the faith I thought I had already exercised was for what? All the times of giving so much to so many; my heart and spirit just sank {I could feel a rebellion building within me but just proceeded on with getting ready for dinner.) I gave my husband a fake smile, and we headed across the street to our neighbors who worked for the Jaguar dealership, so we were being escorted in style tonight! All I wanted to do was get to the restaurant and start pouring tequila down my throat and develop a quick case of amnesia!

We arrived and were seated on the patio. The drink orders started, and somewhere in between, I must have ordered food as well. I could remember the staff of the restaurant coming over to my table with the big birthday sombrero to put on and sing to me. By this time, a few more people had stopped by to wish me a happy birthday. Every time the memory of the cancerous brain tumor entered my mind, I attempted to drink it away. Being a lightweight when it comes to drinking, it wasn't long before I was really lit. We still hadn't told our friends about the brain tumor or cancer. They just thought I was celebrating hard. Our daughter was babysitting their daughter and son, and we had promised to bring them McDonald's McFlurries back, so as we prepared to leave, I really felt just how much I had celebrated!

The world was spinning, and I felt a little nauseated but managed to walk on my own as we headed to their custom-ordered Jaguar en route to McDonald's. As we pulled up to the drive-through window, I could feel a major headache already coming on, and the dry heaves began.

We completed the order and drove off. I can remember us entering our neighborhood, and it did have several hills. Our neighbor didn't want me to throw up in the Jaguar, so he was really giving it gas up the hills, and the dry heaves were getting worse.

I remember getting home and my husband making me kneel over the toilet for a while, and I kept telling him that I wasn't going to throw up. I just wanted to go to bed. Apparently, he got me dressed for bed; and eventually, I got to sleep and remember waking up to a cold compress on my head and him staring at me. I jumped up because it kind of creeped me out, and the banging pain in my head reminded me of my shenanigans from the night before.

The rest of the weekend consisted of the usual: me typing up the programs and announcements for church, running errands for both home and church, attending church, and eating out as my poor hubby had to work on Father's Day. After service, I told my pastor and his wife about the cancer results. They prayed with me and assured me that all was going to be alright!

Before I knew it, Monday was here, and I knew I had to eventually talk to my supervisors about my upcoming need for time off, yet I didn't want to really be specific about it, not even with the church. I knew that "*If God be for me then who can be against me"* (Romans 8:31). I knew that *"the effectual fervent prayers of the righteous man availeth much"* (James 5:16) and *"where two or more are gathered in HIS name asking for anything and believe it, it shall be given to them by my Father in Heaven"* (Matthew 18:20). Of course *"God has not given us a spirit of fear, but a spirit of love, power and a sound mind"* (2 Timothy 1:7). Yet something would not allow me to speak to many of my diagnosis. I knew that not all prayers were righteous, and not everyone was for you, just the opposite of the Word.

In hindsight, I didn't think my faith was in question. I thought God had me tell a select few, those who He knew would play a key role in this testimony no matter the results!.

Later that week, I worked up the courage to tell my supervisor that I would be needing some time off in July for a surgery and was not quite sure how long I would be out, but I would be going to human resources (HR) to talk to them about applying for the Family and Medical Leave Act (FMLA I had chosen to go this route employment wise because in a previous situation four years prior, a great injustice was done to me when I had to be out for medical reasons resulting from a full frontal head on collision.

The following day, my husband and I decided to tell our children. They tried to put on brave faces but appeared to be in shock. They both embraced me tightly. Before I knew it, my husband, the kids and I were locked into an emotional family hug.

I was not sure where the rest of the month went. I guess just the normal grind and trying to keep my mind off the upcoming surgery.

Chapter 14

My kids were raised in church no matter where the Army sent us. They both said they knew that I was strong and that God was going to get me through all of this fine. As I laid in bed that night, I truly hoped that they were right.

The alarm clock went off, are you kidding me? Tuesday was definitely here too soon. We had Monday off since it was a company recognized holiday. The holiday weekend had gone by way too fast. Well, as the commercial said, "Time to make the doughnuts." That did sound good! For once, I was starving in the morning, and the "hot" sign that was totally out of my way was calling to me I assumed like the bat signal did for Batman. I knew what that meant: shower, dress, drop my daughter at school, and carry makeup bag to work with me because Mama would be getting doughnuts this morning!

I picked up a few dozen. Two for the breakroom and one for my office. Oh no, I was not eating out of the same one that everyone else had access to. I had already seen some people not washing their hands after using the restroom or doing other questionable acts! Was I the only one like that? Surely not, I hoped. I was raised that way. I always hated company potlucks! Especially Thanksgiving. Okay, the office would supply the turkey and ham, and everyone else would bring a side dish. Okay, I had done DNA testing and I was mixed with everything ethnicity-wise, but what was the deal with the green bean casserole and stove top? That was some nasty stuff, and it was like Gabriel was going to emerge from the clouds and sound the trumpet if my Caucasians descendants didn't get it.

I was sorry I just had to unload that one. Of course, I didn't like sweet potatoes, black-eyed peas, watermelon, or peach cobbler, so I caught it from both sides! One of my coworkers always laughed at me. We would play the lottery occasionally, and she would ask what I would do if I won the lottery. I told her a month before Thanksgiving I would start buying up all the canned green beans, French's onions, and stove top and then go on eBay and sell them for three times the price with guaranteed shipping/arrival before Thanksgiving and donate most of it to charity. As I sit here almost over fifteen years later I'm thinking that might not be a bad way to invest what money we have now…hmmm.

Where was I? Oh yeah, so I dropped off the doughnuts, and I was everyone's favorite for the day. As they were stuffing their faces in the breakroom, I entered the restroom on my floor with my makeup bag intending to put my face on. I was immediately hit in the face by the overwhelming stench of "number two!" I didn't mean to say it out loud, but I did, "It is just too early for this…you could have dropped that off at home!" I realized I said it out loud and grabbed my makeup bag and made a dash for the door but not before looking under the stall and getting a glance of those shoes so that I could match them up to the owner of that horrendous smell as well to the same scene of another bathroom crime.

You see, for months, someone was going into the ladies' room and urinating on our floor, and when you usually walked into one of the three stalls, there would be urine everywhere! Like someone had a water sprinkler with the rotating sprinkler heads stemming from their bladder. I loved talking with our cleaning lady and felt so sorry for her having to deal with such a mess several times a day. Plus, it was a huge nuisance to the rest of us ladies who had to use that restroom. I always tried to hold my urine or anything else until I got home, but it was a long commute home each day. However, during five days of the month, it was necessary for me to use the restroom there.

After entering the bathroom one day and finding that it had been greatly disrespected again, I decided to post a note on the bathroom mirror asking everyone to please be respectful of others and clean up after themselves.

After a couple of weeks, it continued, and I launched "Operation Urinator: Don't Come Back" instead of Terminator "I'll be back!" The bathroom was located right across from the kitchen, break room, and copy room. I decided to come in early one morning and get a head start on my workload, and then I proceeded to the copy room with a stack of papers in hand to pretend like I was making copies. Every time someone entered the bathroom and I heard a stall door close, I went in, looked under the stall(s), and took note of the shoes. Then after they had exited the restroom, I went in and inspected each stall. We were coming up in the late morning hours, and I knew people would start flooding the kitchen/break room for lunch. I was just about to abort my mission when I saw someone enter the bathroom. I did not recognize her, but I made a note of the shoes and then remembered the last time I saw those shoes and the horrible landfill smell that I had walked in on before. As she exited, I really didn't want to go into the bathroom, but she was out pretty quickly, so I decided to take my chances. I began to check the stall, and bingo. There it was. "The Urinator" had struck again, and I immediately exited the restroom and caught up to her by the stairwell. I said, "Excuse me!"

When she turned around, I saw her badge that we all must have to enter various parts of the facility. I told her that now I had her name and knew that she was the one wreaking havoc in the restroom, and if she didn't stop or start cleaning up after herself, I would look her up in the company directory and report her to her supervisor/manager. She just looked at me in surprise and said, "Sorry."

I went back to my office and looked up her info in our company database. She actually worked on another floor and, for some reason, had been bringing her rude gifts to our restroom. I immediately sent out an email to the ladies on our floor and told them the mystery had been solved and there would be no further problems. Several people tried to get me to tell who it was, but the *"Master Keeper of Others Secrets"* still wouldn't divulge it! I did so In case "The Urinator" had a medical condition, I did not reveal her identity. When the cleaning lady came around for afternoon rounds, I was thrilled to deliver the good news to her as well.

Now I was back in my office with the door pushed up, and I opened one of my desk drawers and pulled out my big mirror and proceeded to put my face on. Not the first time I'd had to do it. With one way in to work, there had often been traffic jams, inclement weather, etc. I had it down to an art at this point, seven minutes tops!

Well, I was getting into my work as my office phone rang, I noticed the area code. It was the same area code of the facility that was treating me. I answered, but it was one of my sisters. I had forgotten that she worked just minutes from the facility. She asked me what I was up to, and I told her nothing, just the same old, same old. She asked if we had plans for the fourth of July, and I told her that I really hadn't even thought about it.

In hindsight, I kind of wished I had lied and said we had plans. Since our mother had died some 14 years earlier, she would host "family" get-togethers at her home. It was usually overtaken by her friends who she had grown up with or gone to school with or both. Family was squeezed in as best as possible. She was always hospitable to us, and I would cook various dishes and bring them. We really just never got any sisterly time. Her friends were always a priority even when it came time to eat, and of course, they had brought nothing but their appetites and often a plus one or more and I really dreaded seeing one of her friends on every family occasion. She was loud, obnoxious and boisterous, but even worse I was unfortunately privy to an awful secret regarding my sister and that particular friend's father (Aaarrgh!!!) and forced to keep it under wraps in an effort to not further distance me and my sister's relationship. Dang why did I always have to carry the burden of keeping everyone's secrets!. I told her we would probably be available. Even though things were as they were, I somehow got some comfort seeing the siblings that showed up as well as driving past the old neighborhood and stopping by the cemetery to visit family that's no longer with us.

We chatted for a few minutes, and I told her I would call her back towards the weekend to see what she wanted me to bring. Fourth of July was still about a week away, but I always liked to plan ahead. The remainder of the week was pretty uneventful. As a matter of fact, everything was pretty much uneventful yet at the same time, hugely significant during this time of waiting for the approaching surgery date.

Fourth of July weekend had arrived, so I cooked up a storm that Friday evening and night as well as all day Saturday in preparation of heading out to my sister's the next morning. I made army-sized aluminum pans of potato salad, arroz con gandules (Puerto Rican style rice with pigeon peas), chess pies, and my pina colada cake.

We left out early the next morning. No room for napping since my husband had packed everything on ice in a cooler large enough to store a body. We arrived in Clarksville around 10:30 a.m. and started bringing things into my sister's house. In spite of the dysfunction that existed, it was always good to see her and my nieces as well as her common-law husband who I had gone to middle school with. My husband and I always stayed in our older niece's room while my daughter slept with my younger niece, and my son slept downstairs on the sofa.

People started flowing in slowly but then steadily and eventually heavily after noonish. My sister was still cooking, and her "husband" and mine were on grill duty as well as setting up the tents, gazebos, etc. My son helped out with the assembling of things as well. Being twenty-two now, I even saw him with a beer in his hand. He wasn't much of a drinker or party type person, but seeing that was just another reminder of how fast time passes us by. When our mother died, my son was only eight; and through the years, we usually went to my sister's for gatherings. Just thinking about how quickly fourteen years had passed was a bit eye-opening.

Within a few hours, the house and backyard was at overflow level. As usual, the family had to fight to get in to eat, to get a seat, etc. Yes it was "friends takeover" number one hundred plus. It was probably best. I had called my sister several months earlier after the brain tumor diagnosis and asked her to drive up to Knoxville (less than three hours) because I really needed to talk to her. This was something I had *never* asked before. However, I was told that it wasn't a good time for her, but she stated she would get back with me. Going on four months, she still hadn't found the time for me. Maybe it was just me, but if someone called and asked me to come and see them because they really needed to talk and this was something they had never done, I would at least be intrigued. There was no indication on her part when she saw me that she even recalled my request from four months prior for her to come see me, so I just carried on as usual.

The next morning, my husband was in the shower, and I was going through my suitcase picking out something to wear for our trip back home to Knoxville and, of course, getting my medications ready to take when like the wind and without notice my sister entered the bedroom and asked what I was doing. I told her I was waiting for the shower to become available, and then it happened!

She saw all the medication bottles and asked me what was going on. Prior to the brain cancer diagnosis, all I took was a daily multivitamin and my birth control pill along with the occasional Tylenol Sinus for frequent headaches and my sinus problems that numerous doctors had been telling me for so long was the cause of my reoccurring and frequent symptoms. I tried to play it off, but unlike some, I had never been a good liar. She saw right through my pathetic attempt at a cover-up, and I had to come clean with her. I told her, "Before I say anything, you have to promise me that you will not repeat this to anyone!" She raised her right hand and said, "I promise, Nese [my nickname that also meant "banner of God"], I swear to God I won't!"

Everything within me was telling me not to tell her, but I took a deep breath and told her that the reason I had asked her to come months earlier and see me was because I had been given a grim diagnosis: chondrosarcoma of the brain. Now she had worked in the medical field in the past and understood what *sarcoma* meant: cancer! She looked at me like never before and said, "You have brain cancer?" I told her technically yes and no. I explained what the doctors had told me: how it started as a bone tumor but was located at the base of the skull. As time passed, it progressed to cancer, and there were pieces of the tumor on the brain. I also told her that it was extremely rare and happens to less than one-eighth of 1 percent of people in the entire world!

(now it is medically stated that this happened to less than 1/16 of 1%). The doctors told me my chances of winning the lottery maybe even twice were far greater than ever getting one of those, and I only had four choices in the US for the surgery and only one choice for the cancer treatment.

She hugged me, and I once again **begged** her to keep her promise and not to tell anyone else, and she once again not only promised **but swore to God on her own life!!** (People, be mindful of your words…they are more powerful than we probably even could imagine!) I told her that I didn't want anyone else to know because I didn't want anyone to worry. That was a lie. I didn't want anyone else to know because deep inside I knew based on past incidents that no one would be there for me. So I figured if no one knew, then I would have no expectation, thus no hurt or disappointment.

This would turn out to be one of the biggest mistakes, regrets, and let downs of my life. (Note to self: always listen to that inner voice.)

My surgery date was coming up on the twenty-seventh of the same month, and I really just wanted to get home and be around my husband and kids. In other words, those people who really loved and cared for me.

The weeks seemed to fly by, and before I knew it, it was time to pack my suitcase (my expected hospital stay could not be determined nor could the success or even my survival of the operation) for the hospital, tie up some loose ends around the house, and head to the hospital. I knew that my husband would be staying at the hospital for whatever length of time that was to be. That was a given, and for that, I was truly grateful and blessed. But I knew my kids ages sixteen and twenty-two would want to be near me as well, so I had asked my sister if they could spend a couple of days at her house since she lived only forty minutes from the hospital as opposed to them driving five to six hours round trip daily to see me. She graciously opened up her home to them. I was truly grateful for that as well.

After all, we were still awaiting to be reimbursed a few thousand dollars in travel expenses from trips made from our house to the hospital since this whole nightmare began so we could not afford to take on hotel expenses for them as well. We had already left messages for the American Cancer Society as well as been told that due to short notice and the long waiting list, the best they could do for us was give us an address to a place in the city of the surgery, and we would have to stop by there the day we arrived to see if they had openings/cancellations. We did just that but were told when we arrived that they had no accommodations. To make me laugh and with quite a bit of truth behind it, my husband said, "I'm glad they don't have any rooms. It looks worse than my basic training barracks." God, I love him!

My sister did remind me that she would not be home to cook for them because she was actually working in the same city (I hope you caught the fact that I said *the same city*) I was having the surgery, and her commute was horrible. I told her that was fine. My son was driving his sister down in his car, and they would have money to eat on.

Chapter 15

Sunday morning July 25, 2010, my family and I got up and got ready for church.

It was extra special not just because it was my last Sunday before my surgery, but also because my husband was able to get the day off from work and would attend church with us as well.

He normally worked Sunday through Thursday from about 9:00 a.m. to 9:00 p.m. He was salary, so you guessed it, no extra pay and of course not at the executive level so overlooked when it came time for bonuses.

Today, none of that mattered. I had called my pastor the day I was diagnosed by the eye doctor with the "wonderful bedside manner," and he came right over to console and counsel my husband. On that day, I asked him to respect my privacy and to not share my diagnosis with the church.

Again I had been let down so many times by people in my life like my family, close friends, and church clergy and members that I just didn't want to go through anymore hurt again.

Also there was always this little voice that would speak to me when things were going wrong telling me that, "Not everyone is for you, so be careful who you share your problems and concerns with." I think it originated with advice that my mother would share with me and all my siblings as we grew up. In hindsight, I now knew that it was a lesson she learned far too often and far too well, and that simply broke my heart and made me miss her so much more.

On the other hand, I was conflicted because the Word of God tells us, "*If God be for us, then who can be against us*" (Romans 8:31). I just decided to have the Pastor tell the church that I had a medical issue that I was dealing with and to be in prayer for me, and every Wednesday night "intercessory prayer/Bible study" and Sunday service, I would go to the altar for prayer.

I followed suit on this last Sunday before my upcoming surgery on Tuesday. This time, my husband and children joined me at the altar! Wow, what a moment! What an unspeakable, indescribable moment! Hallelujah! The Word of God tells us, "*For where two or three are gathered in my name, there am I in the midst of them*" (Matthew 18:20). I certainly felt and knew that in my heart on that Sunday!

I should have also known that the enemy would soon be coming to attempt to steal that Word and joy from me! After all, that is his job. The Word of God tells us, "*Be sober, be vigilant; because your adversary the devil, as a roaring lion, walketh about, seeking whom he may devour*" (1 Peter 5:8).

After service, we gave and received handshakes, hugs, and kisses from the Pastor and congregation, and then we were on our way to grab something to eat. Today, I got a break from cooking my normal huge Sunday dinners. Instead, we were going to one of my favorite restaurants. I loved good Italian food!

We ate till our hearts and bellies were content, shared a dessert, and got the remainder of our food to-go for later consumption. We went home, changed into more comfy clothes, and everyone disbursed to their rooms for their favorite activities.

Hubby and I got the rare opportunity to relax in bed, watch some television, and he even cuddled with me which is not his favorite thing to do. He hated being in bed during the daytime, I really appreciated the sacrifice as well as the frequent embraces of reassurance.

I think we had mutually decided to intentionally not make love the days leading up to my surgery because that reminded me of a send-off which was something I had become too familiar with since my husband's almost -twenty-two-year military career consisted of too many of those!

We had to be at the hospital the next day prior to my surgery. I was to have one more brain MRI performed and to have the fiducial markers placed in my head. This consisted of the nurse shaving twelve spots in my head (based off of the MRI and position of the tumor) and placing the adhesive/fiducial markers on my scalp. As it was explained to me, these markers would be used to help guide the surgeons during the scheduled five hour surgery to ensure that they did not come into contact with vital organs, arteries, nerves, etc.

As she explained that to me and my husband, I couldn't help but realize how invasive and risky this surgery was, but I was not allowing the enemy to steal my peace and joy by instilling fear. At least not on this occasion. For the Word tells us, "***That God has not given us a spirit of fear, but of power, and of love and of sound mind***" (2 Timothy 1:7). He (the enemy) would come for me again in just a couple of hours. After the markers were in position, I was given my pre-op instructions again, and then my husband and I were told to be at the hospital at 5:00 a.m. the next morning.

We left to find a reasonably priced yet nice hotel room in the vicinity of the hospital to settle into before grabbing a bite to eat before my surgery cutoff time. After walking in and checking the price and availability of a few hotels in the area, we found success with the fourth attempt.

Hubby brought in our bags, and I showered and was still able to style my incredibly thick hair to cover most of the fiducial markers! I put on my makeup and some casual clothes, and we decided to grab something to eat near the hospital.

There were several restaurants to choose from "on the strip," but we also had to be mindful of our budget. We were without my income for an undetermined amount of time that had been more than hubby made, plus we were still waiting for the military to reimburse us for so many trips here that included fuel, mileage, meals, and some lodging for months prior. Thank God that since then it has become a government mandated policy that such expenses must be reimbursed within a certain amount of days following timely submission. Plus, the American Cancer Society and every other charitable organization we had contacted, had not been able to help us. Apparently, there were long waiting lists for adults, and my situation and need of treatment had both arose and progressed rather quickly. Our budget was hurting!

We settled into a booth of one of our favorite budget-friendly restaurants, and our server came over to take our drink order. We already knew what we wanted to eat, so we ordered our meals as well. Then I thought to myself and actually said out loud, "Why didn't we just share some thing because I can't have leftovers tonight?"

As usual and what would become one of many lines of encouragement I was to need and get from him, my hubby said, "After you kick that surgery's butt, you are going to be hungry, and this certainly beats hospital food." Did I mention how much I love that man?

As we were waiting for our food, my phone rang, and I saw that it was one of my three sisters calling. It was actually (my now late middle sister; in fact now all 3 of my sisters who were alive during this period as well as my Dad have died.) the sister that I had confided in.

Remember the one who swore her silence to me and to God on her life (there is definitely power in the words we speak and contrary to many unbelievers, we are held accountable for them)! Well, guess what? That little voice was speaking to me again and telling me not to answer.

Regretfully, I didn't obey that voice!

I told my husband it was my sister calling, and I was going to step outside to see what she wanted. We were seated right near the windows facing "the strip," so hubby would have a full view of me.

I answered the phone thinking she had called to wish me well and maybe even pray with or for me. Instead I got the following conversation.

Me: Hello?

My sister: Hey, what you doing?

Me: Just grabbing a bite to eat, and then heading back to the hotel room to get some rest. I have to be there at 5:00a.m. The surgery is scheduled for 6:30 a.m. and an estimated five-hour procedure.

My sister: You're going to be mad at me.

Me: What? Why would I be mad at you?

My sister: Well, I told Dad and a few other people.

My heart sank, and it felt like I was trying to swallow a boulder!

Me: Why would you do that? You promised!

My sister: Well, I got to thinking in case something goes wrong or like you pass away, I would feel really guilty carrying that load of knowledge with me.

Wait a minute, did she just say if something went wrong like I died or something she would be feeling guilty? Hold up, this coming from someone who would not even come to see me anytime I needed her? Someone whose whole life was based on carrying her and our younger brother's treacherous secrets and mess? Oh my God, breathe, Lonnette! On top of that, she was calling me hours before and not even encouraging me (but just the opposite) of what felt like she was wishing death upon me! The Word tells us, "***The tongue has the power of life and death***" (Proverbs 18:21).

In other words, you could speak death or life! You could build others up or tear them down. Wow! This was really happening. The enemy had come for me yet again, and this time, ***harder***!

Me: (I refused to give her the satisfaction of hearing me cry). Our order has just arrived. I have to go. (Note: I wish I had never told her! She was only good at keeping her many secrets.)

This time, I listened to that little voice, and I boldly rebuked the devil right there in that parking lot! When I came back to the table, my husband could tell that I had been crying and sensing my body language, that definitely something unpleasant had just occurred. I attempted to play it off, but he knew. After all, we had been married almost twenty-four years at that point. I lied and told him just the opposite because if he knew that she called to tear me down, it would be on like Donkey Kong. He and I were and are very protective of each other mainly due to situations such as these when people we had loved, given/loaned money to (that was never returned), broke bread with, and shared bloodline and DNA with had used and failed us over and over and over again. Sadly, they weren't through with that yet either!

We finished dinner and went back to the hotel. I washed the makeup off my face since it was not allowed in surgery. We got into bed, and my husband, as he always does, said, "I love you, beautiful!" I told him that I loved him too. We kissed and held each other until the 3:30 a.m. alarm went off. Sad to say that even with the help of a sleep aid, the enemy and that evil phone call had caused it to be a restless night for me and just one of several more to come.

Chapter 16

We arrived at the hospital, and things began to happen so quickly just to slow down later.

Our first stop was surgical in processing in which they did all the normal stuff such as confirming my insurance, name, address, etc. Then they asked me if I had a living will. Funny how in past surgical procedures, how casual that question had seemed before. I thought the same thing when they asked about my religious preference. The final question they asked was did I know what procedure I was having. It seemed like it was the first time I actually had to say it out loud, "Brain surgery/craniotomy to remove a rare and cancerous brain tumor."

Secondly, we reported to pre-op in which I had to pretty much answer the same questions; and afterwards, I was given two bags for my personal belongings and "the famous gown of shame" to change into. My heart sank when I had to remove my wedding band.

After I changed, a nurse was waiting with a wheelchair, and she began to escort my husband and I down to the area in which I would be put in a bed and hooked up to an IV and would soon come to meet a host of medical professionals. On the way down there, she was sure to point out to my husband where he was to wait for me while I was in surgery and showed him the monitors that were in place that would be updated as my surgery progressed. My name was already the first one on the board along with the surgeons' names. There was no status yet since it was not scheduled to begin for almost another hour and a half.

We finally arrived at the room with my bed, and my husband sat down in the chair next to the bed. Immediately, I was hooked up to monitors, an IV was inserted. I also had monitors placed on me so that my heart could be monitored throughout the surgery, and of course, I, once again, got to answer the same questions from earlier. Then each person would leave and pull the curtain for attempted privacy.

During the moments when it was just my husband and me, we attempted to cover our uneasiness with jokes and kisses and talking about all the things we were going to do once I was all better. I had met the anesthesiologist assigned to my surgery, and finally, the lead surgeon assigned (the director of neurosurgery) came in and shook my husband's hand and explained that he was just going to "get in there and get what he could and get out, with no unnecessary risks."

In hindsight, I knew that he felt he wasn't going to be able to get all the tumor, but he was going to get what he could in an effort to prolong my life. He asked my husband and me if we had any questions for him, and we told him no. He reminded us that he didn't see the procedure taking more than five hours, and the otolaryngologist was already scrubbing in. He would be assisting the neurosurgeon with any nerves that might need to be rerouted or things of that matter. After we all agreed to have a good understanding of all that was (or so we thought) to come, they called for the nurses to unhook me from the gadgets there and for the orderlies to come and push me down to surgery. My husband followed alongside the bed holding my hand the whole time until we reached the double doors in which he could not enter.

My husband looked at the neurosurgeon and told him, "Take care of my girl. She's everything to me!"

The surgeon replied, "I promise that I will."

My husband kissed me for what could have very well been the last time, and we both said, "I love you!"

I felt my eyes begin to fill with tears, and I witnessed my husband turning away quickly in an effort for me not to see his tears. It hurt to think that there would be no one waiting with him, since my sister and none of the people she had told were at the hospital or so I thought. I later found out differently.

The double doors opened, and I remembered entering the surgical room. As I looked around, I saw that same bulky time-machine looking MRI machine with a slab for a bed and something that looked like a torture device with clamps from medieval times. I would later learn that my head was inside that device for fifteen (15) hours. That device kept my head from moving during the procedure. That was vital, considering what was being done to me! It was so cold that my teeth started to chatter. The room was full of bright lights as well. (Little did I know how bright of a Light was *actually* there.) One of the nurses brought me a heated blanket, and then the anesthesiologist showed up and began his job. He put the mask over my nose and mouth and told me to take a deep breath and start counting backwards from one hundred. I could remember getting as far as eighty-four, and then it seemed like everything went quiet and dark.

I awoke and remembered hearing a voice saying, "Miss Collazo, wake up. Miss Collazo, can you hear me?"

I felt a little dazed, but I opened my eyes and realized I made it through the surgery. I was still among the living! I remembered saying "thank You, Jesus!" I felt well rested. I would have no idea until a few minutes later just how well rested I was nor how long it would be before I felt well rested again.

A nurse asked me if I needed anything. I told her, "My husband, please."

She advised that he would be back shortly so the doctor could speak to us both. In the meantime, she would be back with some water because she knew after all those hours, I had to be thirsty. My throat felt scratchy, and I was thirsty, but what did she mean by "all those hours?"

As I was pondering that thought, I heard my husband coming toward me. After all these years, I had come to know the sound of his walk and to feel his presence near me. I had not even asked for a mirror or thought about what I must look like after the surgery. My husband entered the room and bent down and gave me such a huge kiss I thought I was going to need that oxygen mask back. He said, "I love you, beautiful!" He looked tired, happy, and relieved all in one. I would soon find out why.

Chapter 17

The head surgeon entered the room, and he said, "It's really good to see you awake. I actually thought you wouldn't make it through it or if you did, there would be major issues!"

I asked him what he meant because he never gave that indication before the surgery. He simply said, "I will get in there, get what I can, and get the heck out."

What he was about to say would rock my world and change me forever!

He took a deep breath and said, "First of all, I want to apologize to you, Efrain (my husband), because I know the surgery was scheduled for five hours, and it took more like fifteen! I apologize because I wasn't able to give them the information to bring out to you, and I know the surgery update board probably just kept reading "in progress." But things happened so quickly that I didn't have time to consult or communicate with you, and for that, I am truly sorry. But I think once I explain everything, you will forgive me and understand why!"

I was lying there thinking, Am I actually hearing him correctly? Only then did I take notice of the clock in the room, and it read almost 12:00 o'clock. I even said, "Well, the clock says almost twelve, so how can it be that I was in surgery triple the estimated time?"

He replied, "It's almost 12:00 a.m. a new day!" I was still trying to process this information, and my husband interjected and said, "Yeah, it would have been nice to have some information/updates. The surgical monitor's status never changed until the surgery was complete, and I was bugging the crap out of those representatives for info!"

What he meant by this was that he had been there for two shift changes which meant three representatives total!

We were interrupted by the nurse bringing me some Sprite and ice. Now I knew why I was so thirsty and why my throat hurt. I had been in surgery triple the estimated time with a breathing tube down my throat for all those hours! I would soon learn that was very minor in comparison to what else I was about to hear was done to me. My husband poured the drink in the cup over ice and put a straw in it and helped me raise up to drink it. As soon as I took a sip, I asked my husband if he spilled some in my hair. In hindsight, I bet he thought I was still a little loopy from the surgery/anesthesia. He said, "No, baby, just take small sips."

The neurosurgeon said that his partner (head of otolaryngology) would be in a little later to explain that sensation I was feeling as well as some other things. The nurse began to take and record my vitals as the head of neurosurgery continued to explain the time issue. He said a few hours in after the craniotomy had been performed, he realized that none of the MRIs (including the one from one day before the surgery) had revealed that the most dangerous part of the tumor had been wrapped around my carotid artery! (That explains the elevated blood pressure and heartbeat sound in my ear, as well as the 6th nerve palsy in my right eye that the optometrist had diagnosed after I made him examine me again). He said, "If I had seen that on the MRI, I would **not** have even attempted the surgery, and you would be living on borrowed time!"

He took a deep breath and said, "I had extracted all the tumor that I could get to through the craniotomy approach, and I just stood back and shook my head and thought wow, there's still an undetermined amount of tumor in there and now I have to close this nice young lady up, and she will either die from the cancer advancing or the tumor wrapping tighter around the carotid artery causing a fatal stroke! All I could hear was your husband saying, ' take care of my girl, she is everything to me!" I found myself dreading to go out and deliver that information to him and you as well (once awake)."

I looked at him and disappointingly said, "So you didn't get it all?"

He said, "No, we got it all. We got it all!" He continued by saying, "I quickly sent pies and slides to the three other locations that treat/operate on this extremely rare tumor, and they all replied that they had never seen one do what yours had done, and had no helpful tips or suggestions for me."

The nurse had finished taking my vitals but seemed to be drawn in to what the surgeon was saying. He took a deep breath and said, "*Accepting that I had no other option, I bent down to close you up, and I heard a voice say, 'Her jawbone is in the way.' I immediately looked up and said, 'What?' Everyone in the OR said no one said anything, so I shook my head and bent down for the second time to close you up. This time, I heard it even louder, 'Her jawbone is in the way.' Once again, I looked up and said 'huh' with everyone in the OR saying for the second time that no one said anything!*"

I looked at him, and it appeared that his eyes were watering up, and then he said, "*So I picked up the phone in the OR and called for my friend who is a plastic surgeon here. As luck would have it, he was surprisingly available to scrub in.*"

I was trying to process all this. Where was he going with this?

He continued speaking, "I called for a plastic surgeon because I didn't want you to have a hideous, jagged scar on that pretty face of yours, so he came down and scrubbed in and made the cut down by the right side of your ear about three or four inches long. Once it heals, it will not even be noticeable. After he made the cut, we broke your right jawbone in a few places, moved it over, and that gave me direct access to the rest of the tumor! I knew under no circumstance could we hit that carotid artery or it would be game over. So I spent several hours carefully untangling, separating, and removing the rest of the tumor from that carotid artery. The surgery was a *complete success*!"

My husband and I were blown away! Even the nurse was just shaking her head.

He went on to say, "It's a good thing that you are such a fighter and a praying woman!"

I was still taking all this in (I remembered saying that was a miracle! I knew **WHOSE** voice that was) when I spoke it, "I told you from day one that *'this sickness was Not Unto Death'* (John 11:4)." What a mighty God we serve!

The doctor also informed me that I did have to receive a blood transfusion. As of today I have had four blood transfusions total. He shook our hands and gave my hubby "a man hug" and gently patted me on the forehead before exiting.

The nurse intervened and stated, "They are preparing a room in the ICU (standard procedure first twenty-four hours) for you to go to shortly, and from there, you will need to get some rest because tomorrow will be a very busy day for you!"

I remembered thinking about Psalm 23:5, "*Thou preparest a table before me in the presence of mine enemies:*

***thou anointest my head with oil, my cup runneth over.*"**
As I reflect back on this, I am amazed at how coherent and how sharp my cognitive skills were/are. After all, my brain had been open for fifteen hours, my jawbone had been broken in several places, yet the Word of God was still in me and with me!

If I could go back in time, I would warn myself that the enemy was extremely mad at me now and to get prepared for him in any and every way known!

I just remembered drifting off to sleep throughout the night and being awakened for what seemed like every few minutes by nurses taking my vitals and checking my cognitive skills by asking me such questions as what year was it or who was our President. However, each and every time I was awakened or my eyes opened, my husband was there; right there at my bedside.

Chapter 18

The next morning, I was awakened for what seemed like the twentieth time since my surgery! All during the night, nurses were in and out taking my vitals and checking my cognitive skills again by asking me what year it was, who was our president, etc.

I can remember being so tired and annoyed yet in a playful mood that at one point when asked what year it was and who our president was, I deliberately answered, "It's 1808, and our president is Thomas Jefferson! Am I still a slave?"

The poor nurse had such a look of great concern on her face. She stormed out immediately to report these findings to whomever should be notified. I started giggling, and my husband said "baby" as he stormed off after her to tell her I was just joking.

I knew that was wrong for me to do, but I was so tired from a very intense fifteen-hour surgery, in pain, and what little sleep I had during the wee hours of the morning had been interrupted over and over by the same questions.

For the record, I have *tremendous* respect for nurses, and I sincerely apologized to her later. However, that look on her face was priceless and will forever be etched into my memory!

Chapter 19

Well, the breakfast tray had arrived, and since I did not get into an ICU room until just before 2 a.m., I did not get to make my own meal selection. Not that it really would have made a difference. We all know how yummy hospital cuisine is.

After I managed to get a few bites of what appeared to be scrambled eggs in me and some toast and juice, funny, there was that strange sensation again like something cold and wet running from the front to the back of my scalp. I also felt the need to use the restroom. I told my husband, and he buzzed for a nurse. The nurse entered the room and said no problem, there was a catheter inserted. I told her that I needed to do number two, which was a really rare bodily function for me as long as I can remember, and she said she would check to see if it was okay for me (with assistance) to leave the bed and use the restroom in the room. I could pull the IV machine in with me because it was on wheels.

She came back minutes later and said she would unhook some monitors temporarily, and she would walk me along with the IV to the restroom. My husband said that if it was okay, he wouldn't mind helping me onto the toilet. He knew I was pretty shy that way. Even after almost twenty-four years of marriage at that time, neither he nor I were the type of couple that deliberately farted around each other or pooped while the other was in the bathroom.

All that was about to change though. He got me settled on the toilet, and there she blew. All that mystery breakfast made an encore appearance but in a very unflattering manner. (If I could speak to myself then, I would warn myself that this was going to be the first of several bathroom accompaniments my husband was to make with me.) Of course, he had to do this for me four years back when I mentioned earlier that I had been hit full frontal head-on and sustained fourteen fractures. When I think of that five-star rated minivan I was in and how it looked afterwards, my Lord, it was **NOT Unto Death** for me that day as well.

I remember how after the wreck my husband helped me bathe and helped me to the toilet. He even had to put a dormitory-sized refrigerator next to my side of the bed and stocked it with lunchables, juice boxes, and other snacks, so I could take my medication and not have to go down seventeen stairs to our kitchen and risk falling and further injury. It was embarrassing how not one sibling came to even make me a sandwich or help me bathe even after what I had done for one of my 3 sisters two years earlier and so much for all three of my sisters in general!

Yet, I could depend on them for nothing! Correction, that was all I could count on them for...to do nothing! I don't know why they seemed to always have it out for me or didn't support me (I have my suspicions though).

Once again, I was left high and dry. I remember as I was recovering, my husband came home from work with dinner and said, "Hello, beautiful. After we eat, I will give you a shower."

I was dreading it that day because it was my time of the month, and I was a heavy bleeder. After dinner, he led me to the bathroom, which was just a few steps from the bed and mini fridge (I managed to get myself off the toilet when he was at work, but there were times I was stuck on that until my daughter made it home from school and helped me off it. With my right arm broken in three places, most of my ribs on the right side of my body fractured in multiple places, and every bone in the top of my left foot and two toes broken, it was very difficult, to say the least.)

As he began to undress me, I started crying. He stopped and asked me why I was crying, and I told him that I was embarrassed for him to see me because it was my time of the month, and he shouldn't have to deal with that. He grabbed both my hands, looked at me, and said, "Look, you have followed me from one end of the world to the other while never complaining. Not only is it my duty as your husband to take care of you, *but it's my honor!*

"Wow, the tears really started flowing then but tears of joy and gratefulness!

Back to the hospital now as I got off the toilet, I wanted to wash my hands. It was then that I saw myself post-op for the first time! I had a scar from the front/center of my hairline curving all the way over toward the right ear, and it was bloody with approximately fifteen staples! My right jaw looked like Marlon Brando on steroids! In fact it set out so far that it startled me! My right eye was bloodshot red and puffy and appeared to be significantly bruised underneath. Looks like I had just gone twelve rounds with Apollo Creed and lost.

I started to cry, and I could remember the doctor telling me how many places that they had to break the jawbone to gain access to the most dangerous part of the tumor. I was grateful to be alive, but I feared being scarred and disfigured for the rest of my life! My husband kept telling me that I was beautiful and that what I was seeing was only temporary. He reminded me that the most important thing was that I was alive and that the surgeons were able to get all the tumor out.

He got me back into bed, and about a half hour later, a nurse popped in and said that I had some visitors who were anxious to see me.

In ICU, the visits were limited to two people at a time for no more than ten minutes. My husband agreed to step out for a while to let my visitors in.

First to enter the room was my sister in which I had confided in and her oldest daughter. To my surprise, they did not gasp at my appearance. Instead, my sister complimented my skin. That was something she had always done. I seemed to have inherited my late mother's skin, and it was flawless. I never had acne or large pores like most of my siblings. Just then, the neurosurgeon entered the room to check on me, and I introduced him to my sister and niece. He told them the great news of being able to get all of the tumor out. He left out the miracle though. He went on to apologize if they had been waiting for me yesterday and for the surgery taking triple the time. My sister said she wasn't at the hospital, but she was awaiting news from my husband. I felt a lump in my throat. Could it be that with the exception of two brothers, all my other siblings lived forty miles from the hospital, and no one was there to wait with my husband! She even worked in the same town as the hospital I was in. Minutes away. Wow!

Before the maximum ten minute visitation was up, she said she had to get back to work but would stop in to see me later; by that time, I should be in a regular room.

That would turn out to be another one of her many lies or broken promises! She worked minutes away from the hospital and **never** came back to see me during that stay or the four other stays in which I incurred post-op infections. Nor did she even drive two hours from Nashville to my house after my releases from surgery and 4 postop infections hospitalizations to offer a helping hand. In the upcoming months, she was once again to break a huge promise to me as well as break my heart. I wouldn't see her again until the *following year*!

Next, my oldest sister and Dad entered the room. My dad made his usual corny jokes like how could I have had a brain tumor with no brain. They too vowed to come back to see me. That would become a lie as well. I didn't realize that this would be next to the last time I saw my oldest sister alive.

My youngest sister was not there, and I wasn't surprised. She had been addicted to crack for over twenty years at that point. I had even raised her eldest son for three years with no gratitude.

I was somewhat surprised that my middle brother wasn't there. Over the years, he had overcome addiction, imprisonment, and some really hard times. I was always there for him emotionally as well as financially. My husband would later tell me that he was at the hospital the day before. He was the only one who showed up to wait with him. Over the years he and I spoke somewhat frequently. I still have every letter he ever wrote to me as well as every picture he drew for me when he was incarcerated several times for years at a time and I always corresponded back with him in an attempt to keep him encouraged during those dark times and also kept money on his books. He did tell me how much he appreciated it. He also told me that with limited resources he often bought M&Ms with the money on his books and melted them down to use as color in his drawings. The day of my surgery he even risked getting arrested for driving on a suspended license. And therefore, he had to leave after the initial five hours the surgery was originally scheduled for. That made me feel somewhat better knowing that my husband wasn't alone the entire time. I will always be grateful to my middle brother for that.

Now my baby brother, I thought this would have been serious enough to warrant a visit from him. After all, hubby and I had helped him out financially several times, hosted him and his plethora of girlfriends over the years in my home, sometimes giving up our own room. He didn't show up after I had been hit full frontal head-on a few years earlier and sustained fourteen fractures that I spoke of earlier or when I had gastrointestinal surgery and my first blood transfusion the year after that. Yet my middle sister could get a hangnail, and he would get to her by any means necessary. I was deeply saddened as well as hurt by him bailing on me yet again.

My mother had passed away fourteen years prior to this, but I knew in my heart even if she probably had been alive, she probably wouldn't have been there for me either. Everyone seemed to think I needed nothing for some reason!

One of the things I would like people to take with them as they read this, is that "strong" people need to be loved, supported and cared for as well. I think that a great deal of people including myself who are classified/labeled as strong is probably because we have had no other options but to be strong in order to survive life's challenges! We pour so much out to takers and forget to set limitations for ourselves. Even the "encourager" needs to be encouraged as well.

You can't keep pouring from a container and expect that it will never run out. Why do people lose sight of something so simple?

It just seemed after surviving crisis after crisis, making straight A's throughout all my years of school, numerous academic and band accolades, scholarships, etc., everyone seemed to think I could handle anything or they were jealous. I thought a little of both!

All those years of excelling in all I put my hands and mind to, my teachers and most friends never knew that I was living in pure hell *everyday*!

Most nights, I would pull the pillow off the full-sized bed that me and my older sister shared; and since I had to leave the blanket on for her, I would enter my closet (we had twin closets in our room), pull down my winter coat to keep me warm, and wait for gunshots or someone to be stabbed as the never-ending arguing, belittling, and abuse continued. *Everytime* I retreated to my closet, I vowed unto God that I would never have a marriage like that nor would I ever expose my future children to that chaos. I kept that commitment to God and therefore He continues to keep HIS to me! At some point I would eventually fall asleep and I would awake with shoe prints on my face from where I had ended up laying on a shoe. My younger sister and brother would flee to our neighbors house for peace in the middle of the night. When my older siblings were at home and all hell began to break out, they had their means of escape. I always felt compelled to stay because I may have to call an ambulance, police department or whatever. I am angry that I was always put in that position, but I understood spiritually why that was.

I could never have friends come to stay the night or even visit me because there was no guarantee when things between my parents would pop off.

There were some good memories but few and far between. As I continued to channel all that dysfunction into being the smartest or the best at what I chose to do, my siblings and I had definitely learned comedy and "playing the dozens" as coping mechanisms to survive each day.

Over the years, I would have to say that in spite of all the dysfunction, my mother and I were extremely close, Or so I thought. The night of my senior prom, my mom and I rented movies and got pizza with the money from my fast-food and babysitting gigs. I had been asked, but I knew that my parents didn't have the means to buy me the things I needed, and I had already been embarrassed in junior high school, which was now called middle school, by wearing a hand-me-down pantsuit and very ugly shoes. A cousin of mine who was best friends with a guy named Jimmy H who I mistakenly assumed was my boyfriend both poked fun at me, and I ended up calling my father to come and pick me up halfway through the dance! It's so strange to me that people think bullying and cruelty came into existence only recently.

Even after my high school graduation, my mother and I went to the movies as I celebrated with her instead of attending various parties. I always had a soft spot for my mom and tried to spend time with and treat her to something whenever I could. In hindsight, I knew she was living a really unhappy life and probably felt trapped. After all, she had started having kids at age 15 and had very little work experience outside the home. However, even with that closeness, my mother would come to hurt me in my adult life as well; by doing things that hurt far worse than the beatings or harsh words and names I was called by her as a child…again hurt people hurt others!

The first time I experienced one of her adult hurts towards me would be weeks (Memorial Day weekend 1988) after I delivered my son. My husband had sent me home from Germany to have the baby because where we were stationed near the German/Czechoslovakian border and along with his regular training and border patrol duties, that, kept him away from me for nearly 260+ days a year, and there was no American hospital on the small military base we were stationed at. When the threat of premature labor and other complications became a risk factor for me and the baby, my husband insisted that I return home. He didn't know but that only made things worse. I began having complications that eventually led to preeclampsia as well as gestational high blood pressure and ended up having to have 19 hours of induced labor with nothing for pain. Even after delivering our son, I kept having bad pain for weeks and finally went to the ER at the military base back home.

My second visit to the ER revealed that I had over 70 pebble-sized stones in my gallbladder. However before the discovery and seeing proof of the stones the military doctor that was on call had asked me how long I had been an alcoholic since my liver function was way off. When I told him that I don't drink and if he would take a closer look at my records before making such a serious accusation, then he would see that I had just delivered a healthy 10 pound 4 oz baby boy weeks earlier. He then just looked back at the records and said, "Oh!" Yep, with absolutely no apology to me for his unprofessional, egotistical, and stereotypical remark/accusation! That eventually led to my first surgery. My gallbladder had gone into shock due to sudden and rapid weight loss (I had lost 74 of the 83 pounds I gained during my pregnancy by the time my 5 week checkup appointment arrived) therefore my gallbladder had to be removed. At this particular time the laparoscopic procedure did not exist but since I was so tiny the scar did not go all the way around my stomach as the approach had been explained to me prior to this surgery. In fact it's only about 2 inches long with two small holes left for the draining tube.

Well, on Memorial Day that same year, (my son was about seven weeks old), and I was sitting at the kitchen table with my mom just shooting the breeze, enjoying an extra day off from work.

Yep, even while in severe pain from the gallstones, I went back to work (full-time) just five weeks after delivering my son. It was hard and emotionally painful but a necessity at that time. My husband and I got married in a private ceremony with a minister and a couple of friends as witnesses. We were not about to ask either side to pay for a wedding, and no one had even given us a dish, spoon, etc., after we married. I mean nothing!

In fact when we moved to Germany, just a few weeks after getting married, we lived in a small apartment in a German neighborhood. The apartment was like a studio apartment, about 400 hundred square feet, furnished, and the only room with a door was the bathroom. The living room had a wall to separate it from the bedroom. But if you were in the kitchen or heading to the bathroom, you had a clear shot of the bedroom. We had not taken our car over there because it was what the US Army referred to as a non-command-sponsored tour. Which meant if a soldier was bringing his family, he was responsible for the thousands of dollars to ship a vehicle and any household goods as well as finding independent living quarters.

The day I first arrived in Germany, after my husband had secured a place for us to live, when I exited the airport in Nuremberg, Germany (my husband, a friend that he had made and his wife had picked me up), and 1 1/2 hours later, we arrived in the little town of Himmelkron, Germany (the location of our apartment), which I later learned was nearly twenty-five miles or so from the base of Bindlach, where my husband had been stationed. I got out of the car and took a step into the yard leading to the one door and one window studio apartment, and my foot sank so deeply in the snow, my husband had to carry me to the door, which was romantic but good grief, the snow was up to my knees, and I am 5'10"!

As I mentioned before that with regular training drills, field requirements, and guarding the German/Czechoslovakian border (yes, 1987 before the East-West German wall came down), a few weeks after getting settled in, my husband was gone anywhere from 240 to 260 days a year! On the days he was home, he had to take a taxi to work, and when our money for that ran out, he would get up a few hours early and hitchhike to the base. I would cry, and he would always hug and kiss me and say, "It's okay, baby. Someone always picks me up."

I knew that we had no other option, such as asking either of our families for assistance. We didn't even have a TV or VCR for the first nine months of us living there. The day my husband came home with a boombox and one CD (Anita Baker's *Rapture*. I was so excited). When he would regularly have to leave for thirty or forty-five days, I would listen to the one American radio station until it signed off around 10:00 p.m., and then I would play the one CD over and over until I fell asleep. I often fell asleep reading the Bible, with the boombox turned down low just so I wouldn't feel so alone or scared. Afterall, I went straight from living at home with a large family and then thrown into what seemed like isolation, especially with no American neighbors and despite having German descendants on my father's side of the family, I did not speak German very well,

I made sure I budgeted accordingly in an attempt to save money for a "hooptie," which is what they called a much older German vehicle that would pretty much be an eyesore but would get you from point A to point B. A great deal of the soldiers had one either as a primary car (for lower-ranked soldiers or a second car for higher-ranked or two income family soldiers). I took a taxi once a week to the base and walked to the bank, post office, the tiny commissary, mailroom (to check for mail or packages and to also check the job openings for the tiny base), and then the little bookstore. I would treat myself to one book or a magazine a month. Besides the Bible I had packed in my suitcase and the book or magazine I would purchase and having no television, I did a lot of reading and mostly repeated reading.

Like I said, the apartment was nice and clean and furnished. We just had to buy cookware, glasses, etc. Before my husband reported there, just about two weeks after we married, I started buying dishes, silverware, towels, etc.; pretty much anything I could mail to his company APO box/mailroom. However, I was not aware of the wattage difference, and we later learned that we needed transformers to convert the wattage of simple things such as my curling iron, toaster, etc. Transformers (where you could plug American devices into the transformer and then plug the transformer into German outlets). They were super heavy and were definitely not cheap. We ended up on multiple occasions catching a taxi to the gate of the base (taxis were not allowed to come on to the base) and walking in the knee-deep snow and going to Army Community Services (ACS) on the base in which we could borrow things like transformers, cookware, etc. We pretty much needed everything because none of the items I had shipped two months prior to my arrival had shown up yet. So, hubby and I would be walking in the snow with groceries, cookware, transformers, etc., to the gate as we awaited another taxi to take us and the items home.

Our apartment was under a detached garage. Our land-lord and his family lived in a very nice home right next to us. When he opened the garage, we would practically drool looking at his cars (Maserati, Porsche, BMW, Lamborghini and Mercedes). When he would leave for work in the mornings and start up one of his vehicles, our apartment would smell like fuel for at least an hour. Several months later, on one of my weekly visits to the mailroom, I saw a "hooptie" for sale in the parking lot. It was $400. It was a silver Fiat, probably fifteen years or more older. It had several dents in it and, like most vehicles in Germany at that time, was a manual transmission. Something I had not had the opportunity to learn well. I wrote down the number and went to a pay phone to call it immediately. I did not want to miss out on this opportunity. I knew my husband knew how to drive a manual transmission, and he could stop taking taxis and hitchhiking to work. However, there was no answer, so I took a taxi back to the apartment and decided to call that evening from our apartment. We had a phone in our apartment, but at that time in Germany, there was a meter installed on the side of your phone which showed your usage. It actually moved as you talked, even if you were just calling next door, also on incoming calls as well. Not that we're getting many of those! So, I had to keep phone calls to an absolute necessity. Well, I finally got an answer when I called later that evening and learned that it was a soldier trying to sell it because he and his wife had been using it as a second car, and his tour was nearly up at the base. I told him my husband was on border duty, but he assured me that the vehicle would meet our needs. He put his wife on the phone for her and I to set up a time to meet and take care of the transaction.

We agreed to meet at the location of the car the next day (I know I had to break my once-a-week-cab rule I had for myself but for a good cause), and she took me around the small base in it to show me that it started, stopped, and ran. She said she had learned to drive a manual transmission in this same car. I gave her the money, and she gave me the keys and title, and I took the "For Sale" sign off it. I walked over to the driver's testing building and picked up a study guide for the German driver's license test. I had already heard that it contained two hundred written questions and then an additional forty question test to test our ability to interpret what the various German traffic signs meant in English. I was so excited about my husband's return and excited to take the German driver's license test. Yeah, I was geeky that way. Since my hubby and I had a valid American license, we wouldn't have to take the road test. That was a great relief for me. Something told me to stop by the mailroom even though I had just been there the day before, and low and behold, there was a government job on the base listed that I felt I qualified for. I picked up the application from the mailroom (it was super long) and took it home to complete. The job would actually be at ACS! The very place that had loaned us so many items.

The day finally arrived when my husband was to return home. He got a chance to call me the night before his return, and I told him that I would meet him at the base. He said that there was no need to spend money on a taxi going to the base since he was pretty sure that he would need to take one home. I made up a story that I was already going to be on the base, and he said okay. I was so excited that night that I could barely sleep,

The next morning, I walked over to his unit about ten minutes prior to them arriving back from border patrol. After he was released, we ran to each other and embraced. He was so handsome. He said that he was going to ask some guy in his unit for a ride home, and I told him not to worry about doing that. He looked confused and then stated, "What are you up to?"

Just like he does to this day, he can usually tell when I'm about to surprise him. I told him that we should go check the mail, and he agreed. When we got to the parking lot, I pulled out the keys and showed him that we were the proud new owners of a 1970 something, "trash can appearance" Fiat in the lot. His face lit up, and he opened the trunk up and put his gear in, and then he walked over to the passenger's side and opened my door. He then got in, and after a few tries, it started up, and he said, "Baby, I appreciate you! Thank you!" Something he still does on a daily basis, whether it's for doing something big or just making a simple meal. He is amazing! We've been through our ups and downs just as any other couple, but I am truly grateful to God for giving me such an amazing man. We met as teenagers, eighteen and nineteen, and were married at twenty and twenty-one. I guess you can say that we molded each other and truly grew into adulthood together while defying all marital odds that were against us:

1. Different cultures
2. Age
3. Military MOS (combat status) that caused him to be away months or over a year at a time from me.

Things were beginning to look up as I did get the job at ACS that I applied for. When interviewed, the manager, JoAnn, and another employee named Karen said that they recalled how pleasant I was every time I borrowed or returned something to the "lending closet," and they were very impressed by that as well as my educational achievements and office skills. We ended up naming the car Oscar because it looked like a famous trash can character by that name.

My husband and I took the driver's exam. We both passed. The instructor said that I missed one, but I was confident that I didn't; he wouldn't even show me the one he said I missed. And my husband missed four. I laid it on thick with the bragging rights for a while. He taught me how to drive it, and we would leave a little before 5:00 a.m. to make sure he made it to 6:00 a.m. formation and physical training (PT). He would bring his uniforms and toiletries with him, shower, and change after PT. I would have enough time to return home, shower, and get dressed for work, which started at 8:00 a.m.

It started getting to the point where it would not start up on its own, so we always parked on a hill. Even when my husband was out on training maneuvers or border patrol, there were a few guys in his unit, and they would meet me at my job at 5:00 p.m. each day and ask me if I was ready for my push to head home. When I got home, I had learned how to park on the hill so that the next morning I could put it in neutral, let it pick up speed, pop it into second gear, and be on my way.

Then, a couple months later, I learned that I was pregnant for the first time with our son, who is currently a Fourth Generation Army (Special Forces) Warrant Officer. Once I learned that I was pregnant and told him when he got back from a forty-five day stint away from home, he said he didn't want me to be driving the car back home by myself in the mornings that I would drop him off a couple of hours before I was due to work. So I started parking on a hill up from the building I worked in and sleeping in the car until it was time for me to be at work. Eventually, I was given a key to the building and ran the lending closet pretty much on my own as well as office manager duties. This was a blessing because now I could drop my husband off and go to work and stretch out on the couch that was there, until people started arriving and did not have to wait in the cold car for a couple of hours with blankets and pillows. Since I purchased the vehicle in late Spring, we knew it didn't have air conditioning, but the defrost had started not to function. In fact, I had to carry a large thermos of hot water that I boiled before leaving and would roll down my window and throw it on the front windshield whenever it became too difficult to see the road.

Then the heat went out. Germany is definitely not the place after September (at least where we were) in which you didn't want to be without heat. Plus, a hole had developed in the front passenger side floorboard, and a mouse that we could not catch had set up residency in our vehicle. I remember almost running off the road one morning as it decided to cross over my feet as I was driving. Oscar held up long enough for us to be blessed enough to purchase a new vehicle. By that time, the car had started jerking and gyrating something awful when you exceeded 40 mph. Some of the pregnant ladies that I had met who were overdue often asked for a ride in Oscar to see if it would induce their labor. I am thoroughly convinced that it was successful with one of the ladies, or either it was purely coincidental that even though she had no Braxton-Hicks or regular contractions before riding in Oscar earlier that day, she did go into labor that night and had her baby. Eventually, we sold Oscar to a soldier who was a mechanic by trade for $100. Something tells me that over thirty-eight years later, Oscar may still be on the roads of Germany. It seemed to be one of those things that could survive the apocalypse.

Oh yeah, back to "The Hell House" on Memorial Day of 1988, my dad had entered the room about three times in a fifteen minute span opening the refrigerator and just gazing up and down the shelves for something to eat. I knew better than to say anything. Over the years I had learned both of their behavior patterns when they wanted to violently engage with the other, He wanted to pick an argument so that he could leave the house and be with a lady who lived around the block from our home in which he would continue to cheat with until my mother's death and marry her a few months later.

Both parents were habitual cheaters, tit for tat. Not sure who started it but I did know that my father cheated with women he worked with, neighbors, my mother's cousin, and even my mother's only...1'11 just stop there. My mom did her thing too. I don't know why they remained together but I also loved them both and hated being put in the middle of their dysfunction! Once again with my birth placement I saw the things my older ones witnessed and the ones they missed out on by escaping home and the ones below me were too young to recall certain events. I guess that's why I've always had a nurturing and protective spirit because I was probably the only 4 or 5 year old that knew how to heat a bottle on the stove, test the temperature, hold the baby, feed the baby, burp and change it! My mom had taught me these things so that I could help out with my younger siblings since everyone else was away from the house during the day and I was the "go to" whenever my Mom needed to take a break to shower, catch a quick nap or "entertain."

Well, after the third time of him coming in scanning the shelves of the fridge, my mother said, "Lonnie, you know it's the same little stuff in there that was there when you looked five minutes ago." Just then, I heard my son crying and knew it was feeding time. I went to change my seven-week old son's diaper and then came back with him in my arms in the kitchen to make and heat up a bottle for him. It had been really hard on me and my baby. He wouldn't breastfeed, and my breasts had become engorged. Often, I would be running a fever or had lumps running up and down my breasts and arms. I would wear three or four nursing pads at once on my breast and would have to change them within the hour. Since I had been discharged from the hospital, it was too late for me to get the shot to dry up my milk supply, so the hospital informed me that I would need to wrap my breasts in Ace bandages to stop milk production and eliminate any stimulation to them. Well, my husband returned to Germany, so no problem with that order. However, even the water from the shower would cause milk to continue to produce and flow, so I switched to mostly baths and wrapped my breasts in Ace bandages for months before the milk completely stopped producing. Plus, my son's formula had been switched three times, and he finally was able to tolerate the soy-based formula, which was super expensive.

Nonetheless, he still weighed in at a whopping twelve pounds and two ounces at his two-week checkup, and he was taking eight ounces of formula every two hours! My mother told me to start giving him a little bit of infant rice cereal in his evening bottles, and I had to slightly enlarge the hole on one of his bottle's nipple. By this time since I was supposed to be living at home until my husband completed his tour of duty, I had bought myself a new bedroom suit (something I had never had) and a bassinet and crib for the baby. In fact, my husband and I had bought everything for the baby because not one family member thought enough to give the baby a gift nor even threw me a baby shower so that others could give me a gift. I was a hardworking and respectful married woman who conceived during marriage, and you would have thought that I was a hell-raising teen mom that got knocked up by some random. I will never understand that. I was down the hall from my parents and always got up with my baby even though I had to be up at 5:00 a.m. to feed and dress him, pack his bag for day care, drop him off, and get across town to work. Yes, daycare. I'll come back to that.

My dad came back into the kitchen again, and my mother stated, "Why don't you just leave and go be with her. It's obvious what you are trying to do," (referring to his cheating and current mistress at that time Debra).

Then the profanity from both sides began, and I told my mom to hush because it wasn't worth it, and that after I fed the baby, I would go buy some barbecue for us all. The moment I said it wasn't worth it, my dad came back into the kitchen, and my mother was sitting at the small round table in a chair closest to the sink and about a foot from the stove. He tried to strike my mother with his huge fist, but since I was at the stove with the baby over my shoulder when he swung at my mother, and she moved, he missed my infant son's head by inches.

If he had connected, I was sure my son would have been killed. I said, "Dad, what are you doing? You almost hit the baby!"

He then came at me and slammed me into the sharp edge of the formica countertop (As I was still holding my infant son) back first (I still wear that scar today), and somehow, I got away and called 911 as I observed that he was now choking my mother. When the police showed up, I was bleeding from the injury to my back. I told them what had happened, and they asked my mother if she wanted to press charges, and she declined! They recommended that she get a TRO (temporary restraining order), and then they asked if I wanted medical attention for the bleeding injury on my back or to press charges, and I said, "Yes!" They cuffed him, and on his way out, he called me a stupid bitch and told me that I better be out of his house when he returned.

One of the officers asked if I had any other place to go, and I explained to him that I didn't and the situation about my husband and how I was paying to live there until he returned. Plus both parents were always hitting me up for more money throughout the month that I have never got back. The officer stepped away for a little while, and when he returned, he said he had contacted the military base where we lived right outside the gates from, and I should pack a bag for my son and me because a military police officer would be showing up within the hour to take me and my son to a safe place.

I did just that, and before they arrived, I took the filthy barrels of trash from the backyard and dumped them into his precious car with the "coffin lined" velvet seats and rolled the windows up all the way so it could marinade in the 97+ degree heat! I'm not proud of that because that was an indication that the cycle of dysfunction was trying to carry over and I later repented and gave him the money to have it detailed. My mom and dad were good people, but severely damaged from traumas of their own. That's why it is so important to communicate, get help early on, pray and rebuke those generational curses!

The military officer showed up and took me and my seven-week old son to a shelter for battered women. My son and I had to stay there for a few weeks. For the safety of the other women and children staying there, I was not allowed to call anyone from the shelter nor give them the location! I had just paid my dad the money to stay there for the upcoming month, and I had no money for a deposit, first months, rent, etc. I had gone back to work when my son was five weeks old and was still awaiting my first paycheck. All this because my mom chose him over her welfare, my welfare, and my child's welfare! (That was adult hurt number one.)

My infant son and I lived in the shelter for several weeks, and as I mentioned before, we were not allowed to make any phone calls from the shelter or to even tell anyone where the shelter was located to protect the other victims there. There was a shared shower with several stalls as well as a bathroom with a few toilets and petitions in between. Because my son was an infant, I could bathe him in his portable tub in our room and did so every night before bedtime. I hated taking showers in places like that because it was just like a locker room, no privacy, so I went out and bought me some flip-flops and would wait till late at night and take my shower after my son was already asleep. Sometimes, I would go down to the shared TV room where the other victims were and we would engage in conversation or simply remain quiet and watch whatever the first person there had put on the television.

I was better off than most of the ladies in the shelter because I was already working (I was fortunate enough to return to my 911 dispatcher (love the irony) job that I had vacated to follow my husband to Germany shortly after we married. I just had to wait until I made a couple more paychecks to have money to put down on a place for me and my son to stay, and I did just that.

This was my first time living away from home without my husband or on my own, so I wanted to live somewhere safe and familiar. I ended up moving in the same neighborhood I grew up in that was conveniently located to the daycare in which I took my son to when I went to work because for some unknown reason, my mother would not watch my child even though later she would practically raise my youngest sister's first child and even raise one of my first cousins' daughters while she was deployed in the military. Being a first-time mother, I really wanted my mom to watch my son, plus it would be during the hours that my dad was at work. I wouldn't have to worry about volatile situations, but for some reason, even though I offered to pay, she wouldn't do it. (Adult hurt #2) It all worked out though because my son was placed in the class of a very loving and trusted neighbor "Ms. Peggy" whom we lived a few houses down the street from me when I was growing up.

I should have had the strength or courage to tell my husband before he sent me back to that "hell house" about what I had experienced for over twenty years, and I know we would have figured something else out for sure, but I was just too ashamed and too embarrassed like most victims are. I was also pretty sure that if I had not been thrown back into that environment, my first pregnancy would not have been classified as a high-risk pregnancy because I otherwise had no other diagnosed health issues. Instead, I developed preeclampsia and gained eighty-three (135 lbs to 218 lbs) pounds, but after delivering a healthy ten-pound-and-four-ounce boy at the same hospital in which I was born, I had lost seventy-four of the eighty-three pounds in five weeks (right back into my size five pre-pregnancy clothes). That would later come back to haunt me as it threw my gallbladder into shock as I mentioned earlier. I developed gallstones at age twenty-two and ended up right back at that same hospital to have my gallbladder removed just a few months later!

The American Red Cross was able to get my husband home in enough time to see me go into surgery and to help with our son and my recovery {because I'm pretty sure no one else would have) for a few weeks afterwards even though I was in the same town as my mom, sisters, etc. I knew no one would come to care for me or the baby after surgery, plus it was not laparoscopic back then so that caused several limitations on my part and the need for help with an infant!

Thank You, Lord, that this sickness was **Not Unto Death**! Since I was sending my husband money back to Germany to eat and live on, I had to let him know that I had moved out and that our expenses had increased but made up an excuse that the house was just too crowded.

Things were really tight financially. I knew there were plenty of days my husband probably went hungry while I was trying to get me and our son established, but on our limited phone calls, he would never say anything negative.

When I got my third check, I was finally able to leave the shelter and ended up getting an apartment two blocks from my parents' house. I thought I should be close to someone I knew because unlike all my other siblings, I never shacked up with anyone nor lived on my own. I went straight from home to marriage to Germany a couple months later.

The third and final time my mother hurt me as an adult was when my husband and by this time, two children had been relocated from our second tour to Germany {what's up with me having a baby everytime we went to Germany) to Kansas; my husband had to leave for training in California after we had only been there eleven days and knew no one. I became violently ill and suffered severe migraines that caused me to throw up and couldn't stand any light. At that time, my son was eight years old, and our daughter was 2 and a half. My son was checking in on me as I crawled to the bathroom to throw up or asked him to bring me a drink to take something for the fierce headaches and telling me not to worry because he was taking care of his sister. Bless his heart, he was feeding them cereal, lunchables, and peanut butter and jelly sandwiches. My husband finally got a chance to call home a few days into this mystery illness, and then and only then, did I break my own separation rule (I had always remained brave during our letters and very rare phone calls), but this time, I started crying and told him how ill I was. I knew that I had to because I feared for the safety and welfare of our children if I continued on this path of illness.

He told me to stop crying, that it was going to be alright, and that he was so sorry. He then advised me that he would call me back in a few minutes. I didn't know what he was planning, but I was hoping he would be able to return home. Within thirty minutes, my husband called back. He said he didn't have long to speak and that he had jumped in front of someone else in line in order to call me back. He went on to say that he spoke with one of the guys/friends he had made in his unit and that his wife would be calling me shortly. We said, "I love yous, and I hung up to await the call from his friend's wife.

Another few minutes passed, and the phone rang. I answered. On the other line, there was a lady who identified herself as Barbara Dickerson. She was a wonderful woman with five boys who took me to the ER on three occasions, where I threw up all over her van each time. After packing up belongings for me and my small kids, she allowed me and my children to stay with her for thirteen days until I recovered from something the doctors could never diagnose. God bless Barbara Dickerson wherever she may be now. This Sickness was **NOT Unto Death**.

Wherever Barbara Dickerson is, I want her to know that I am eternally grateful to her. Just one of many examples of how strangers and non-family members were and are better to me and us than actual blood family!

The sickness went on for seventeen days, and doctors were never ever to give a diagnosis. During this time, I had called and asked my mom to come and help me, and she said she couldn't go anywhere because my grandfather (her father) was going through cancer treatment and she had to chauffeur my grandmother and him around. This was true, however, imagine the surprise when I called my older sister, who was living in Kansas City at the time, to see if she could come help me and my mother answered my sister's phone.! When I asked her what the heck, she said that my sister really needed her because she was falling apart from divorce proceedings initiated by her husband. Really? Really? I mean REALLY!

A few months later, my grandfather passed. A very recent, recovering me and my two children drove from our house to Kansas City to pick up my sister and her daughter to drive thirteen hours to Tennessee for the funeral. Even though I had just recovered from the "mystery illness," my mom gave my sister and her daughter the good bedroom while me and my children were put on a thirty-plus-year box spring and mattress, the same one from our childhood, the same one my oldest sister and I had shared since I was five years old, which became the one that my youngest sister and I shared since I was twelve and she was two years old, and she had peed on every night before I got married and left home. Wow, wow! I know my mom loved me but she just didn't realize that I was always being casted aside because apparently I was an honor student and didn't get into trouble. It's kind of like working a job these days: it seems that you get punished or not rewarded for your great work ethic. We took pictures as I got ready to drive us all back. I didn't know that would be the last time I would see my mother alive!

She died three and a half months later, somewhere between Thanksgiving night and early "Black Friday" morning, "in her sleep" and discovered by my dad. That's one of the stories that we were told by my Dad. Over the years I have had the same dream/vision of what really happened to my mother. Each time I am shown that she did not die naturally! The details surrounding my mother's death changed so many times that I really wanted an autopsy, but I didn't have the right to insist on one because she was still married to my dad, and he insisted that he was sure it had something to do with the enlarged heart she had been told that she developed from a bacterial infection a few years prior. He said he guessed the medication wasn't working. Something just didn't sit right with me about her passing. She had sounded so great on the phone two days earlier. She had called me from my grandmother's house and asked me to Western Union her some money because she was cooking Thanksgiving dinner for a multitude of people, and I, of course, obliged. I told her that I would see her for Christmas and that I loved her very much (I realize those were my last words to her and that gives me some peace), and she sounded happy. In fact, the last letter I received from her a few weeks before her death was yet another request for money. She stated, "I need it to buy some food for the house. Your dad is so involved in cheating that he hardly gives me a dime and often I go hungry."

I felt sad, mad, and confused all at the same time. It bothered me so much that I even showed it to my husband when he got home from work. He just shook his head and told me to send her the money.

Plus, on the morning of her death our home in Kansas had three levels. All of the bedrooms and one of the bathrooms were upstairs on the third level. On the second level was a huge living room/den combination, and the downstairs level had a half bathroom, dining room, separate kitchen, and laundry room. I had not wanted my newly divorced oldest sister in Kansas City, Missouri, who lived alone with shared custody of her daughter, to be alone for Thanksgiving, so I looked beyond previous hurts and invited her to Fort Riley, Kansas, where we were stationed at the time. They had arrived early in the afternoon of Thanksgiving Day, and I had prepared a feast. After dinner, we cleaned the dishes and put away the leftovers.

We all watched some television and then decided to turn in for the night. My husband and I had decided to give her and her daughter our master bedroom, and we slept on an air mattress in the living room. That way, our kids could stay in their own rooms. At exactly 5:12 a.m., I arose out of a very sound sleep and sat straight up and looked all around the room. It was as if someone had shaken me, but next to me, my husband was snoring very loudly; that was something that continued to worsen throughout his military career. So I crept upstairs and quietly opened all three bedroom doors and found each person accounted for and sleeping peacefully. I thought it was so odd. I was sure that someone had shaken me and woken me up. I eventually went back to sleep for a couple more hours.

We got up and had a quick breakfast in order to catch some Black Friday deals. The phone rang as we were about to head out the door, and when I answered it, an uncle of mine (one of my dad's brothers) asked me if he could speak to my sister. I found that a little odd since he called my house asking for her. In a matter of minutes, my life was about to change forever! My sister came upstairs a couple of minutes after I had handed her the phone, and I will never forget the expression on her face when she entered the room. Before she could say anything, I immediately yelled, "No, no. My mother is not dead!"

Don't ask me how I knew. After all, I had gone back upstairs to grab a different coat for my then three-year-old daughter, and my sister was down on another level of the house. What makes it even more strange is the time I was awakened also turned out to be the time my mother was pronounced dead after repeated attempts at resuscitation at the military hospital that both I and my son were born.

I was transported back to the present time when my children entered where I was in an ICU hospital room, and all was right again. I told them that I would be going to a regular room either that day or tomorrow, and they said they would be back to see me then. I hugged them as tight as my body would allow and told them to drive carefully back to their aunt's house.

By this time, I was getting a little worn out, and I was glad to see my husband as he re-entered the room and helped me get as comfortable as possible. I dozed off for a few minutes only to be awakened by a nurse coming in to take my vitals and to let me know that I would be moving to a regular room later that day. She also brought a lunch and dinner menu to me to select my choices for those two meals. My husband read the choices and filled it out for me. It was difficult to see out of my right eye. {I would later learn why.)

It seemed like I had just closed my eyes when I was awakened by the arrival of my lunch tray. My husband got me all propped up and then uncovered the tray and began to get me situated when a nurse stuck her head inside and said, "After lunch, your room should be ready and sometime that day, a therapist would be by to further evaluate your cognitive and motor skills." I finished my soup and fruit cup and drifted off to sleep.

I was awakened a few minutes later by the second surgeon, the head of otolaryngology. He complimented me on how well I appeared to be in spite of everything. I laughed and told him that I bet he used that line on all his chondrosarcoma cases.

He went on to tell me that his role in the surgery was to monitor and reroute any needed nerves or things of that sort. He said, "Young lady, I want you to know that you have been completely rewired! You may have noticed some little quirks already, but there will be more that will surface in the upcoming days and weeks. Some will be permanent and some will not."

Immediately, I thought of how it felt like someone was pouring water down my scalp every time I drank something cold. I voiced that concern, and he said that was one of the examples he was speaking of as well as me not having any superficial feeling on the right side of my face yet feel ing three different types of pain underneath the surface. At times, it felt like bee stings, sharp pains, as well as pain that felt like electrical currents running down the right side of my face in which the broken jawbone had been fractured in several locations during surgery.

Sadly today, more than fifteen years later, I still experience those same side effects and more. Sometimes, my scalp gets so hot that it develops sores and is even warm to the touch. At the same time, sharp, stabbing pains can be almost unbearable. Also since the brain biopsy was done through my nose, that means I can only allow saline water up that nostril and nothing else! I remember the first time I forgot those instructions and was washing my hair in the shower; when I leaned back to allow the water to rinse the shampoo out of my hair, some of the tap water got up my right nostril, and the pain literally made me fall to my knees in the shower. It felt like I had been bludgeoned with a hard and sharp object with great might.

As of today, I have had two very invasive and unsuccessful sinus surgeries to attempt to alleviate those problems and restore the sinus cavity. When I get too hot, too cold, or overexerted, my right nostril leaks clear fluid but not brain fluid. I wonder if the surgeons anticipated that when they did the biopsy. I have considered trying yet another sinus surgery, but I just don't know if that one would be successful as well. Honestly, those surgeries are really hard on me, and I'm not feeling it right now.

Plus my dad, who I had been cooking for and traveling to Nashville and Clarksville Tennessee for all of his V.A (Veterans Affairs) appointments and surgeries unbeknownst to me, had died the day of my second post brain tumor sinus surgery. Since I was in so much pain and unable to talk, my husband attempted to call him for those two days as I asked him to. I spoke to my dad everyday and had become concerned because we were unable to reach him, but we planned to try again after my follow up visit that morning.

At my follow up visit, as I was waiting to be called in from my vehicle, because at that time we were on covid protocol, a friend and former childhood neighbor called me and asked how I was holding up. At that time, I assumed she was talking about my sinus surgery and as I began to tell her about my surgery, she stated, "Oh my god! I can't believe it! They did it to you again! Honey, your dad died two days ago!"

I guess the emphasis should be on *"again"* because this had happened to me three times before in which I had learned either through third parties, (outside family) or social media of the deaths of two of my sisters and one grandmother.

I immediately called my dad's phone. One of my first cousins answered. I asked him where my dad was and he said "oh my god! I'm over here with your two brothers and they both said they called and told you that your dad had died (no missed calls, messages or voicemails on either phone plus they had my childrens' phone numbers also) two days ago." He went on to say, "I should have known something was wrong because you would've been the first one here." Each brother was in the background saying they had called me and told me and I just got mad and hung up the phone. My husband had been listening to all of this and was really ready to drive up there and do bodily harm, but he knew he had to take care of me from the second sinus surgery. I was running a low grade temperature, in horrible pain and the world was on Covid shutdown!

A short while later, I called a lady that would come over and help take care of the house and check on my dad and his second wife sometimes. She stated, "I'm so sorry, I didn't have your phone number, and 2 of your brothers and cousin are over here taking everything of your dad's that isn't nailed down." She told me that she would call me back in a little while because they were making so many trips to the vehicle that they should be done in a few minutes. When she did call me back, she said she went into my father's room and looked around and noticed that his coin collections, all his family photos dating back to the 1800's (These would include relatives from three different countries), jewelry, and even his expensive suits, shoes and hats were gone. Everyone that knew my dad knew that he dressed very stylish, and I felt like I was in a nightmare, and at the same time I felt nauseated and as if I was going to faint. My Husband told me to calm down and put me in bed. My phone rang and he saw that it was the same lady calling so he answered and I saw him walk out of the room with my phone. He returned a few minutes later to check on me, I asked him who was calling me, and he told me that it was nothing to worry about right now. I knew by the look in his eyes that he was attempting to protect me as he always has, and does. I asked him once again who was on the phone, and he said it was the same lady calling to tell me that they had returned for my dad's vehicles, but were only able to take one.

When my mother had died many years earlier and my father had bought a double plot and double headstone (one for my mother and one for him). On one side of the double headstone it had all my mothers information, and on the other side it had all of my dad's information, excluding the month, day and year of his death, that would be filled in when that time came.

Since the time had come, I called the funeral home, which our family normally does business with, and when the receptionist answered, I told her who I was and asked if I needed to bring a suit and other clothing items for my dad to be buried in (because I knew all his other clothes had been taken), and what the receptionist said next absolutely floored me and sickened me to my stomach. She said, "Honey, I can't believe they didn't call and tell you that they had arranged to have your dad's body picked up this morning and he has been cremated!" Sometime later, a memorial service was planned but I'm not sure exactly who was included in the planning, but I do know that I wasn't. By me not being included most of the information on the obituary was incorrect and they even omitted my oldest sister (who was technically a half sister but my dad had legally adopted decades prior) from the obituary and program.

Since we were still in covid protocol, I was advised by my ENT surgeon that he strongly recommended I not expose myself to large crowds. However, unbeknownst to them, they had no idea that I had no intentions of attending, yet hours before the planned ceremony, I received a threatening text from someone texting from my nephew's phone stating, "No one gives a f_k about you being your dad's first born and if you show up, we're going to jump you!" The text also asked, "Did you get that ugly dent in my head fixed yet?" (referring to the bones I have missing from the craniotomy). I have an indention on the right side of my head near the forehead. Over the years, doctors have offered to fill it in, but I really don't want it to be opened up again, and for the most part people don't notice it unless they are petty or if I point it out. I also consider it my battle scar that symbolizes giving God the glory. I don't know or care who the cruel lost soul was and once again I put it in the Hands of God, this too was *Not Unto Death!*

I found it strange that the cruel text had come from the nephew who had stolen all of my well hidden prescription painkillers ten years earlier on his only visit to my home and weeks later my sister/ his mother (who had a known opioid addiction) was found dead at her kitchen table from an apparent overdose and I had even paid half the cost of her funeral with a temporary headstone that thirteen years later still has not been replaced by a permanent headstone even though she has two grown children. So whoever it was that sent that text their time would have been better used handling that situation instead of being evil! I posted a screenshot of the text on Facebook to see if anyone would recognize the phone number or who it came from. Other people apologized to me for having to experience that type of behavior on top of learning of my dad's passing from a non-family member.

Until recently, I had not spoken to those involved in the shady events relating to my dad's death, and I had no intention of doing so, until I recently saw two of my three brothers at the burial of my final sister who was the baby of us seven kids and neither apologized but yet read scriptures pertaining to unity and spoke about breaking generational curses. SMH. I tried so hard to save my baby sister. I prayed, sent money as often as I could to keep her off of the streets, and prepaid her heart and asthma medications for her at the pharmacy to ensure she was getting her medications. I chose that option because I felt sending money would allow for her to use the money for her addiction.

There were times in which she weighed so heavily on my mind and spirit, that I would take to social media to inquire if anyone had seen or heard from her, because like so many addicts, she would disappear for various periods of time.

I finally had to realize that there are very evil people out there and some of those people share the same DNA, but it's not for me to handle. It has been placed in the Hands of God. I continue to thrive in health and other areas. I have a great network of support from my husband and children and great friends and I know this too was *"NOT Unto Death"*!

Chapter 20

Now let's get back to 2010. That evening, I was moved to a regular but private room. Shortly after settling in with some of the comforts from home such as my favorite pillows and comforter my husband had brought me, I was waiting to hear what the next steps would be in my road to recovery. Just then, there was a knock at the door and enters a hospital employee who was introduced to me as a therapist who was there to check my cognitive and motor skills.

As she read through my chart, she giggled and called me a little jokester. I knew then the nurse had documented my remark I made about it being 1808 with Thomas Jefferson being our President and asking if I were still a slave.

Then she blindsided me with a question that no one had bothered to ask me since the surgery: can you tell me the earliest memory of your life?

I began to feel my eyes well up with water, and it felt like a family of frogs were in my throat. The very things I hoped would no longer be part of my memory were still there! In fact, I felt like every traumatic event was actually in the room with me and unfolding in real time.

Allow me to explain. At age four, I had two significant memories:

First, the one and only birthday party I was ever given in my life. Well, at least not again until I was forty. I recalled how my childhood nemesis (let's just call her A-Lee)-who bullied me and who outweighed my frail and anemic frame by at least thirty pounds-had pushed one time too many! After a morning of nonstop and unfortunately, routine arguing and profanity, violence had broken out between my mother and father, and the party almost never happened. By some miracle, it did, and I was not going to be bullied on my special day. Being the middle out of seven kids (well, only six at that time), these types of events (parties and gifts) were virtually unheard of or nonexistent due to the constant economic struggles I would experience until I left home and even afterwards.

Somehow, my mom had been able to get me a new yellow cotton/linen dress with white flowers embroidered on it. That was also a rarity in our home because our wardrobes usually consisted of hand-me-downs or clothes that Miss Josephine from church would bring to my mother at least twice a year that were being discarded from a wealthy Caucasian family she cleaned house for.

As the kids began to arrive, the party hats and favors were being distributed. I was so excited. I wore my cardboard cone-shaped birthday hat that had the rubber band that went under the chin to keep it secure with great pride and excitement, and then it happened. My nemesis arrived, and I could not believe she was there. However, she did live only a few houses away, and I was pretty sure she wasn't invited, yet she reached for a hat and a bag of party favors.

As she put the hat on her extra-large head, I heard the infamous snap. Her rubber band popped, and immediately, out of all the kids there, she came up to me and pushed me. She then said she didn't care if it was my birthday, she wanted my hat. She said I thought I was so special because I had long hair and that I was light-skinned. I didn't even know what that meant then, but know that same remark was used on me well into my adulthood. (My father had blonde hair and blue eyes until he was six years old and was often mistaken for different ethnicities. I guess I tended to take more of his physical characteristics.) Nonetheless, no one was going to take my special day away. To my surprise, I socked her a "good one" right in her big belly and she immediately doubled over in pain. My grandfather saw it all unfold and was laughing like crazy. I guess during the tussle, my dress sustained a grass stain, and my mom discreetly pulled me to the side and nearly yanked my broomstick of an arm out of its socket and then slapped my face really hard. She didn't even want to hear my explanation!

I, of course, now know where both my mother's actions, the rest of our family members' reactions, and even my nemesis's actions came from: a very dark and hopeless place of hurt that so many of us had/would come to experience in our lives that would take us all down very different paths in life. Oftentimes, hurt people tend to hurt others or displace their anger and frustration. Sometimes intentionally as a release of their pinned up pain and anger, and sometimes unintentionally, something like a vicious cycle or generational curse that needs to be broken.

After somehow pulling myself together and wiping my tears away, she gave me a warm embrace and told me to go have fun, and I watched her walk away with my younger brother on her hip and enter the house to breastfeed my then youngest sister who was an infant at the time. My only younger brother was two and a half years younger than me, and my then baby sister was barely over thirteen months younger than my brother and almost four years younger than me. This happened to my mother a few times in which she became pregnant again before the current child was a year old. My younger brother and sister had no idea of how much I often watched them, fed them, diapered and protected them. All of my other siblings were in school and when my mom needed to take care of certain things, I was pretty much all she had. I was given that role of caretaker and protector at a very young age.

I had three half-siblings above me. My father had married my mom when he was twenty-one and in the Army, and my mother was twenty-three. My mother was already a mother to three kids by three different men by the ripe age of twenty, and my father often, if not daily, reminded her of that fact. I was my father's first child of what would eventually be four with my mother.

When I returned from beside the house, my grandfather saw me holding my arm; and being so fair complexioned, he knew immediately that I had been crying. I remembered him hugging me and slipping me a shiny half dollar coin in my hand. He also told me I did a great job on A-Lee! He was such an awesome grandpa and which I later learned had overcome a lot of demons to become that warm, loving and patient person he was.

Immediately, my memory brought me to the second event in my life at age four that changed me forever! It must have been about four months or so later. My older siblings who were like thirteen, twelve, and eight were all at school, and there was a knock at the door. I recalled my mother was at the stove making me and my little brother oatmeal and nursing my sister. She told me to pull back the curtain to the back door and see who was knocking, and I did just that. I came back and told her it was Mr. Bobby Hatter who was the landlord of the tiny house that my two parents and us six kids were occupying and the only other house on that street besides my grandparents home. I remembered her saying, "I wonder what he wants." She told me to let him in and to tell him that she would be there soon, and I did just that. He always seemed like a nice man to me and kind of reminded me of my grandfather with similar build and obvious Native American bloodline somewhere in his genes.

As my mother finished nursing my sister, he sat down at the table where me and my brother were eating breakfast. He asked me how old I was, and we talked about me starting kindergarten in a few months. After a few minutes my mom entered the room and told me to go watch my younger sister who she had placed in the crib of her and my dad's room, but I was always a very curious person and very mature for my age. Little did she know after I peeked in on my sister, that I was in the hallway listening to their conversation the entire time.

Mr. Hatter went on to tell my mother that he thought he could catch Lonnie (my dad's nickname and who I was named after, hence, Lonnette) before he left for work. My mother said he had left early that morning to pay a bill before work. Mr. Hatter went on to say that my dad had not paid the rent in three months and month four was coming due and that he understood that he had a lot on his shoulders with a big family and the only one working, but he needed his money as well, and if my dad did not get him the money, he would have to put us out of his house! I was looking at my mother's face the whole time as I had never seen that extreme expression of shock on her face before but little did I know I would see that same expression in just a matter of hours. As my mother had learned to do so well, she pretended all would be well, and she would get with my dad after work. Mr. Hatter thanked her and said both his apologies and thanks.

My dad had served in the Army and even served two tours in Vietnam, one before I was born and one after I was born at Fort Campbell, Kentucky. I was the only child in our family born into the military since my dad concluded his enlistment after his second tour to Vietnam. He was a a very hardworking man who often worked two jobs since it would cost more for my mother to pay for childcare than to work outside the home. With that being said, he also controlled all the money and gave my mom a household allowance for food, clothing, and school supplies/fees. I could remember my mom always looking forward to Spring and Summer because she could stretch the allowance further by Granddaddy (her father) keeping us stocked with vegetables he grew yearly after his early retirement and meat that he had actually hunted and killed or fish that he and my grandma, whom everyone called "Little Mama", had caught as they fished almost every day during the summer except for Wednesdays and Sundays because they were both very active in our, at that time, little country Baptist church that would eventually grow, grow, and grow!

My grandfather was a deacon and the volunteer janitor and maintenance man until the church, many years later, was able to throw a little something his way. My grandmother was a mother of the church, head of the ladies chorus, and primary "shouter" when the Word was being preached or halfway through her solos. She was also a great prayer warrior and though she seemed to favor the boys over the girls, I learned a lot from her!. My mother was in the ladies chorus and later, the mass choir who actually recorded an album titled *"Rivers of Joy"* in the '70s. Both my grandmother and mother had wonderful voices and performed solos on the album. My grandparents were in church every time the doors opened; my mom was there as much as she could be with so many kids and only the one car in our family. Oftentimes, I would ride with my grandparents and loved it when we visited other churches for second service on Sundays.

Our pastor lived a few streets over, and his daughter and I were friends, and my brothers were friends with his two sons. On several occasions, my mom would let me ride with our Pastor and his family to other churches. Looking back now, I can see that I had a thirst for the Word and a purpose. I just didn't know then what it was.

My mom would sometimes hug me and call me her miracle baby because I was the smallest baby of her then six kids and was born six weeks early. Also at the age of fourteen months, my mother was hanging out laundry, and my older siblings were supposed to be watching me since we had an incredibly high porch at that particular house. I was told that one of the neighbors came over and started tickling me and saying how cute I was, and I lost my balance and fell over six feet to the ground. My head hit a brick that was surrounding my mother's flower garden and was cracked open, bleeding profusely with brain matter exposed. Everyone knew I would not survive that but God! I was told that there was no time to even administer anesthesia and that a medical party of four held me down while the surgeon on call sewed my head up. From what she told me in my teenage years, it was pretty much a "lets see if she makes it through the night" situation regarding my chance of survival. It was **NOT Unto Death**.

Even as I write these words, I am fully aware that the enemy had been after me since I was in my mother's womb and he would continue to be after me!

Now back to that day in 1970, My mother went on with her daily chores; my older siblings made it home from school. It was dinner time. Dad wasn't home yet, but that definitely wasn't the first time, so my mother held dinner an extra hour and then told us to go ahead and eat.

Before I knew it, it was bedtime for me and my younger brother, and my mom had got the baby to sleep and was still awaiting my father's return to discuss the rent situation. That night, I just couldn't go to sleep; at that tender age of four, God was keeping my eyelids and ears open for a reason. I was about to learn a lesson, a coping mechanism, an excuse, and a channel for all hurt and frustrations I had endured and would endure throughout life as well as the reason that kept me from fleeing the home in later years when things between my mom and dad would become so volatile!

It was a little after 10:00 p.m., and everyone was home sleeping/accounted for except for my dad. That's right, at age four, even though there were no digital clocks as of yet. I could tell time, and I heard the news blaring through the walls from my parents' bedroom television that was on the other side of me and my other siblings' room.

I heard my dad's car pull up into our gravel driveway, and I heard my mother's angry footsteps headed down the hall to confront, not greet my dad. This would be a changing point for me, my older siblings, mother, and father forever. I often wished I had been one of my younger siblings so I would not have witnessed and would not recall over and over for a very long time what was about to happen as well as what would even continue to happen!

I heard the back door open, and my dad came inside. My mom asked my dad where he had been because, once again, he had come home late smelling of liquor with a volcanic lava of profanity and violence that was about to erupt and spill out. My dad told her, "Don't worry about it, bitch, and then pushed her out of his way as I stood in the hallway watching and listening as I often did while the others remained sleeping because it had become second nature in our household for them to fight all night!

As I now know, my dad had returned from his second tour to Vietnam and had what we know now to be PTSD;

and to add fuel to the fire, he had turned to liquor and gambling at a local pool hall in the neighborhood as a coping mechanism.

My mother continued to ask him where he had been and why he smelled like liquor and then the worst question of all: where was his paycheck because she knew he had got paid that day. He called her out of her name several times and pushed her again. My dad was about 6'3" and probably about 230 lbs, and my mother was 5'3" and maybe 150 lbs; she still had a little baby weight on her from giving birth earlier in the year. Hardly a fair fight to say the least. Shouting matches and physical abuse were nothing new to me, but what was about to happen would be heard around the world-at least mine!

My mom told my dad that Mr. Hatter had been by the house and said that the rent had not been paid in three months and was threatening to put us out. She told him that she knew he had drunk and gambled it away. My dad had hazel eyes, but I could usually tell what kind of mood he was in due to the green flake in his eyes. Call me crazy, but his eyes always looked olive when he was not wanting to be bothered or in some cases, looking for confrontation. It was at that very moment he lifted my mother off her bare feet and slammed her against the wall and had her in a choke hold. She was trying to pry his hands away from her neck, and I could hear her choking. I ran up to my dad and started beating him in the back of his thighs and yelling for him to stop. That was all I could reach at that age.

Eventually, one of my older brothers woke up and joined in with me beating my dad and yelling for him to stop. To this day, I don't understand how my other siblings slept through this. My brother was four years older and was very strong for his age. He was able to hit my dad in the back repeatedly as I continued wailing at his legs, and eventually, he released his "death grip" from around my mother's neck.

Then I saw my mom stumble and run into the room across the hall and went into the closet and came out with a rifle that my grandfather had given my oldest brother for the purpose of game hunting with him. My dad pushed me and my brother across the hall and ran into the room. By that time, my mother had taken the rifle down off the shelf and had put a shell in it.

At this point, my father attempted to take the rifle away from my mom, and they began to wrestle for full possession. The trigger was on my mother's side, and the barrel was on my dad's side. The next thing I knew, both of them had fallen to the ground, and then I heard the loudest noise I had ever heard! It sounded like the cannons I had heard in movies that my dad used to watch or the tank rounds when I got to witness my husband in a training drill! Then I heard my dad yell, and immediately, there was more blood than I had ever seen in my life…even to this day! There were pieces of flesh, clothing, and God knows what else plastered against the wall.

I immediately sprang into action and ran into our small living room that was also where our one rotary dial olive green telephone was located and dialed zero. There was no 911 then. (Yet I would become a 911 operator on three occasions in my adulthood.) The operator came on to the line, and I said verbatim: my name is Lonnette Liggins, and I live at 109 South Oak Street, and my phone number is 648-3279 (no area codes were needed at that time unless you were calling long distance), and I needed an ambulance for my daddy because he was dying, and I needed the police because my mommy killed my daddy!

Eventually my dad came home from the hospital and even in 1970, miraculously they were able to save his leg from amputation for nearly 50 more years. We remained in that little house until 2/3 of the way through my 5th grade year. When my parents purchased their first home and moved to another school district, I lost the security of my friends and knowing all the teachers and was immediately thrown into a new neighborhood, new school, new people, but the same old dysfunction and hell at home! The school system did not change for my older siblings.

Sadly, this wasn't the last time they would make such a drastic move at such a crucial time in my life!

It had been forty years, and I could still remember every word, the address, and even the phone number. By this time, I had moved a few times with my family and had lived all over the world with my military husband. Yet I could remember every address and phone number, area code, street address, zip code, or in some cases, country codes in which I had ever resided!

My mind continued to rewind like an old VHS tape, and I just kept recalling things that I really didn't want to. I guess numbers have always been my thing. History (because of dates) and Math always came easy; that along with this often photographic memory had been both a blessing and a curse at times. After all, I started preparing both grandparents and parents' tax returns in the eighth grade. Though I thoroughly enjoyed school and always excelled, yet something was missing that made me think of middle school, or as it was called, junior high school. In seventh grade (my first year of junior high), I selected "beginning band" for one of my classes. I was always too tall for cheerleading, already near my final ending height of 5'10" still wearing my long, thick hair in two braids or ponytails because it was too much for my mother to handle. Also, I was not popular, nor did I feel pretty enough. I was usually wearing hand-me-downs of some sort and I definitely did not have enough clothes, I didn't even have enough to not repeat outfits in the same week. So I wouldn't be able to pull off that image that was often associated with cheerleading. Plus, I was already part of the drill/dance team called the New Providence Mustang Pacers. We got to wear our little hoodies like white shirts, red athletic shorts with a white line down each side, and cheap white tennis shoes with red stripes. To my surprise, my parents managed to get me the shorts and shoes, and the tops were from a sewing pattern that our instructor, Mrs. Owens, had picked out. My now late friend and classmate Virginia had her sister make my top for me, and my dad paid her; I'm sure, at a discounted rate. Virginia's dad, Mr. Frank, and my dad were both very good friends. I loved it when my dad took me with him to Virginia's house. She had her own room, amazing dolls, her own radio, and so many awesome things. It was decorated like a princess with a canopy over her bed, and her quiet and reserved mother, Ms. Jessie, was always so nice to me. She would bring us cookies and milk or Kool-Aid into the room for us to enjoy from a very young age; back then I often wished for my friend Virginia's life.

The drill team got to perform at pep rallies (I'll never forget our routine to that popular song "Flashlight" by Parliament, in which we incorporated actual flashlights into our routine, and the lights were even dramatically dimmed in the gymnasium for that performance) and some games and that really made me take notice of the band that was performing as well. Also, I come from a very musically inclined family, both vocally and instrumentally gifted. I was so excited to learn how to play an instrument and be part of something to which I felt I truly belonged. Plus, it would be another outlet (at that time, I had no idea how much of an outlet) to deal with the dysfunction at home. I chose the trumpet initially until my mother said, "Child, your little skinny self don't have enough wind in your body to play a trumpet! Plus, girls don't play trumpets." So, I then chose the flute.

For some reason, it intrigued me. I later learned that it actually took more wind to play the flute than the trumpet. I also remember the band director we had. Her name was Pam Hofe, and she was petite and had a Dorothy Hamil-like haircut, and she definitely had an authoritative-like presence about her. She demanded respect, and she earned and got it. All I needed now was a flute. My parents priced them, but they were too expensive. Mrs. Hofe allowed me to remain in class, and I learned how to read music and practiced fingering the notes on my imaginary flute. Sometimes the girl next to me (I think her name was Teresa) would wipe off the mouthpiece of her flute and allow me to attempt to play the notes, scales, or arrangement of music we were learning that day.

Another school year went by, and before you knew it, Christmas break of my 8th grade year (the last year of junior high school, which would turn to middle school the following Fall) was upon us, and I was sad that I would not be in band or school for a few weeks. I hated being at home. Most times, it was so volatile, and somehow, I became the "secret keeper" for my parents' indiscretions and other things. As I think about it now, I realize how cruel it was for them to put me in that predicament. That's why now I am such an advocate for monogamy and later would stop covering for people's indiscretions. That trait and decision cost me various sibling relationships and apparently fake friends as well. After winter break, we returned to school. I still remained in the band into the eighth grade, still with no instrument.

This time, I was in an intermediate band. Sometimes it was embarrassing to still not have an instrument, but I just felt like that was where I belonged. Then a few days into the second semester, as I was leaving the band room, Mrs. Hofe called me into her office. My heart was beating so fast. I thought she was going to tell me that I couldn't remain in class. I knew that would devastate me. Instead, she told me that she had been approached by the mother of one of her advanced band students and was told that her daughter no longer wanted to remain in the band, and she wished to sell the flute. Oh my gosh, I was so excited. Mrs. Hofe wrote down the contact information for me to give to my parents. The clock could not move fast enough for the school day to end for me that day.

As I mentioned earlier I could usually tell when it was safe to approach my father by the color of his eyes. When he was mad, his hazel eyes would take on a more greenish appearance.

Sometimes, when I wasn't sure if it was safe to ask for something or if I couldn't see his eyes, all I would do was say "hey, Dad," and he would turn around, and then I would judge by the color of his eyes whether it was wise to ask for something or to save it for another time by saying nevermind.

That evening, to my surprise, he was quite approachable; he even called the parent about the flute who was actually a lunch lady at our school, and they agreed on a price. Apparently, my dad was to give me a postdated check to give to the lunch lady, and she would bring the flute the next day. I was so excited I could hardly sleep that night!

The next morning, I took the check to the lunch lady during breakfast so that I would have the flute for my band class later that day. I usually skipped breakfast even though I was on the free lunch and breakfast program. We had different colors for the free lunch tickets and breakfast tickets that indicated who paid and who was on the free lunch program, and more often than not, I would skip meals because I was way too embarrassed to present my free lunch ticket in the presence of other classmates or friends. If there were a day in which I found myself very hungry, I would wait until the end of the line to get my free meal tray; and by that time, lunch was almost over. That morning, I waited till the end of the line and presented the lunch lady with the check that my father had given to me for the flute. She punched my ticket and told me to go ahead and take a seat, and she would go retrieve the flute and bring it to my table. And naturally, I chose the table closest to the lunch ladies' register and eagerly awaited her return! A few minutes later, she returned with the Artley brand flute (one of the best brands), and I felt like it was Christmas, only better I guess because I actually got what I really wanted! I immediately opened up the case, and for a moment, I forgot where I was and started playing scales and notes that I really had not had the opportunity to do before then. I was so excited and so engaged that I didn't realize I was playing out loud and that most of the cafeteria was looking at me until the principal walked by and told me to "put that thing away" and that "the cafeteria was made for eating, not entertaining!" At that moment, I could not have cared less about the laughter! I was not embarrassed! I was too exuberant and overjoyed, so the laughter bounced off me like the dodgeball did off the really obese kid in my gym class! Finally, I could actually participate in class and practice at home!

That morning, the hours and minutes crept by at a snail's pace until it was time for band class! I got to class earlier than usual and took my place in the front row and assembled my instrument. A few minutes later, Ms. Pamela Hofe stepped up onto the director's podium, then raised her baton and began to lead us in various scales as a warm-up to our sheet music. I will never forget when she looked out into the audience of us budding musicians and saw me with the instrument raised and playing my scales! She gave me a wink and smiled really big! That was a day I will never forget! Sadly, it would be followed by another day I will never forget! You see, having that instrument gave me a whole new identity, a confidence I'd never had before! Even though it was technically another hand-me-down in my life, I knew it was something that would forever be mine and only mine! It was something I didn't have to share!

So about ten days later, I went through the lunch line with my free lunch ticket and tray and was among my friends and classmates with my newfound confidence and completely without a care when that same lunch lady looked up and saw that it was me standing in front of her and said in a loud, no, make that an extremely loud-voice that seemed to echo throughout the cafeteria that my father's check bounced and that he better call her as soon as possible and make it right or she wanted the flute back ASAP! I just remembered feeling like I just swallowed my heart; as a hush fell over the usually loud cafeteria, I mumbled, "Yes, ma'am." If that wasn't bad enough, she followed that remark up by saying that my free lunch ticket needed to be renewed! I was well aware of that, and she knew I was. I had only been doing that all eight years of my school career.

In hindsight, I wondered if she was a person who had been hurt and had felt the need to hurt others or in this case, me. Who knows, she might have just simply been mean! Lord knows that both types exist!

I walked to the nearest empty table and poked at my food. Needless to say, I couldn't bring myself to eat anything. I did manage to get a couple sips of chocolate milk in me in though. After all, I needed something to wash down my heart and the lump of disappointment and embarrassment I had just swallowed. I wanted to run off and cry so badly, but one thing I had learned from my mother was never let others see when you hurt! Instead, I said something comedic, which was another coping tool I perfected at a very young age. That quality of learned behavior would become a two-edged sword as I grew older. However, that day, I was hurting in a way I never hurt before; and if I could have wished for any superpower, I would have definitely wished for invisibility!

When my dad got home that night, I didn't even bother to look at the color of his eyes before telling him what had happened to me earlier that day! I saw him go into his bedroom, and I heard him talking to someone on the phone. I guess, eventually and somehow, it all got figured out, and I was able to keep my flute and that would turn out to be a true godsend or perhaps a sort of saving grace to help me escape the hell I was living more often than not and to deter me from falling into dire situations and traps that some of my other siblings unfortunately did. The rest of the school year went off without a hitch. I guess the only complaint I would have was that my parents never attended any of my band functions that year. I had received the flute too late to be in the Marching Band, but I was still on the drill dancing team and Pep and Concert Band. That summer, new laws came into effect, and it was voted in most cases, nationally, that junior high school would now become middle school with grades six through eight and high school would now be grades nine through twelve. So instead of being in the ninth grade and ruling junior high school, I would now be a freshman peon in high school-yay for me!

They had built a brand new high school in my hometown or I guess I should say in the country because it was out in the middle of nothing but cornfields (some of the same ones my parents had once raided) and one little gas station/convenience store that led to the interstate. It was called Northeast High School, and our mascot was the eagle. I was guessing because of the nearby military base, the 101st Airborne Screaming Eagles that was my dad's Army alma mater and where I was born. Out of the four kids my mother had by my father, I was the only one born into active duty military and born at the Fort Campbell Blanchfield Community Army Hospital that would also later be the same hospital that my son would be born into several years later.

So before we exited the eighth grade and the last year of junior high school, we had to choose our schedule for the upcoming school year; and naturally, I chose Advanced Band! Advanced Band was the only level of Band offered at the high school level because normally, most people had three years of band entering high school as opposed to my half of a semester of actual playing time, but I did not let that discourage me or instill fear in me succeeding.

I received the marching band music, prior to exiting the eighth grade, that was going to be played during the football game's halftime show at my upcoming high school and began to practice immediately. At that time, I had no idea that we would not be able to use the clipboards to attach our music to our instruments as we made the various formations during the halftime show as I had observed other bands do. In other words, the music had to be memorized as we executed the steps and formations!

That summer, we auditioned for our chair placement. I was so nervous because I only had one semester of active band as opposed to most people's three, four, five, or six years depending on our high school class, i.e., freshman, sophomore, etc., because of the new school and new zoning laws. Our school was new to everyone and affected all four classifications. Most of us were being separated from most if not all of the classmates we may have been in school with since elementary school. We had auditions and to my surprise and great pride, I still made second chair in the first section! Which equates to the number 3 ranking over others with far more experience. We had a very talented band and won several competitions and even went to the Orange Bowl Parade our first year in Orlando. So that spoke volumes to the amount of effort I and others put forth in such a short period of time. Auditions were followed up by both a one-week-long band camp in which we met our band director, Mr. James R. Morris (aka Jimbo as his precious mother and then wife Marjorie, who trained our majorettes, called him). He was a short man even in his platform shoes. He reminded me of Peter Cetera (former lead singer of the band Chicago). He demanded our best and he totally earned my respect forever and, would become a very significant part of my life as well as various other band members. We practiced hard and heavy in the extremely brutal heat that July brought and everyday after school rain or shine! One of my earliest, proudest band moments was when Mr. Morris was telling us to arch our backs as we made a certain design on our make-shift football field during the first selection, and he must have noticed my 200% effort and though he didn't know my name (come to think of it, he didn't know any of our names since he was a brand new teacher to the area), he said, "Everyone, look at her (referring to me) and do it like she is doing it! "I beamed with pride! Hey, I had to take my wins where I could get them.

I had always been able to succeed at or accomplish anything I applied myself to. Over the years, my straight A's seemed to come almost effortlessly. I truly believe that to be the result of channeling the hurt, rejection, and dysfunction into something positive. I've noticed that what people are exposed to for a long time will result in one of two things: either repeating the cycle or breaking the cycle (good or bad); all I had to do was study some. By the end of the week-long band camp and with the practices in between the start of the school year, we had all memorized and learned not only the music, but also our formations as well. We were issued our uniforms but had to buy our shoes and that made me nervous to go home and ask for that money.

So I was fortunately able to get several babysitting gigs, and that was one good thing about living close to a military base. A lot of the Officers' wives were very social and were always looking for an economical (okay, cheap) source of childcare. There were a lot of military personnel, and their families lived in our neighborhood or very nearby and through word of mouth, I was able to pick up a lot of business before school started that year. I also babysat in my neighborhood and tutored my across-the-street neighbor's daughter, Angel as well. Her mother, Bonnie, told me in my adulthood that Angel would not have been able to make it all the way through school if it had not been for me. That was a very rewarding moment. Therefore, I made enough money to buy my own shoes, and that made me proud! Throughout my high school years, I was very high in demand for the babysitting gigs since I not only watched the children, but also cleaned their houses as well because my mother never tolerated a messy house. In fact, even our beds had to be made and rooms had to be cleaned before the 6:20 a.m. bus arrived on school days; and during off time, all our chores had to be done before we could go outside and play. My mom said that all the dishes had to be washed and rinsed in nothing but pure hot water from the sink. You better not turn on that cold faucet for anything, and our electric stove burners had to be pulled out and scrubbed after each use. After a family of eight or nine ate, you could imagine the number of dishes and cookware that had to be cleaned, dried, and put away.

In hindsight, I knew if my mother were alive today she would be diagnosed with OCD; I'm afraid I inherited some of those OCD qualities as well. My mom was an awesome cook. She used the homegrown vegetables from my grandfather's garden and sometimes, the meat that he had got from hunting. The only time I really caught a break were the mornings where we simply may have had oatmeal or cold cereal for breakfast. My mom would repeatedly ask my dad for a dishwasher, and he would laugh and say she already had 1, 2, 3, 4, etcetera, counting all us kids as dishwashers! My only older sister was about nine years older than me and own her way out of the house by this time, and my youngest sister was ten years younger than me, so it usually fell upon me and occasionally my middle sister, who was four years younger than me, to do the dishes and fold laundry as the boys were in charge of the outdoor work.

That August, school started, and the new high school was so far away from where we lived that our school bus came at 6:20 a.m. to get us to school in enough time for the 7:30 a.m. start time! If we missed the school bus, we were just out of luck because we only had one vehicle at that time, and my father used that for work. You better not call and tell him that you had missed the bus. Plus, I was the oldest in school at this point (my older three half siblings had graduated, received cars, and were on their own for the most part, coming and going as they pleased).

Anyhow, I was always sure not to miss the bus because I wasn't about to miss Band for anything! My parents did not make it to any of my Marching Band events that year or any year as a matter of fact apart from the annual Christmas parade, but I still excelled. It wasn't until my sophomore year in which my band director did not realize that I had only one-half semester of band under my belt prior to getting to high school. That year, I auditioned for and made the All-state Band and earned the "Most Improved Band Member" Award at the band awards banquet that my parents were unable to attend toward the end of the school year.

My parents were usually not present at any of my events or award ceremonies. I would usually catch a ride home and rush into the house to show my parents whatever award I received. In hindsight, I believed Mr. Morris sensed that there was something going on at home because I can remember him coming by in his "National Lampoon" station wagon and picking up several of us kids on weekends and taking us out for pizza or to the movies or simply to the park just to talk. There were several times when we were on the road for football games, and I would be afraid to ask for money to eat on, and Mr. Morris would always give me a couple of bucks to get a hot dog and soda or something when we stopped at fast-food restaurants on the road. But he would attempt to disguise it by saying, "Hey, Lonnette, can you go pick me up a drink and get yourself something while you're at it?"

I remember one time in which we had been selling candy to sponsor an upcoming band trip, and I had really hustled and canvased several neighborhoods by foot and sold several cases of candy to sponsor my trip so there wouldn't be any out-of-pocket expenses for my parents.

However, I did make the mistake as I often did with my babysitting money, and against my better judgment, I loaned it to my mother when she asked though I rarely received it back. She said that she needed to buy some food for the house and other items. I imagined that was true since my dad did have her on a strict allowance, and she had to practically beg for anything that exceeded that allowance, but as the deadline would draw closer and closer to turn in the money and/or the unsold candy, I would continue to ask her for the money back. I had been elected Treasurer that year in band, and while I was busy accounting for everyone else's money they submitted to me, it would be greatly embarrassing if I didn't have my own money that I was responsible for. Every time I asked my mom for the money, she would tell me not to worry and that she would get it to me. Finally, the night before the deadline, I asked my mom again for the money, and she said she would give it to me in the morning.

The next morning shortly before it was time for the bus to arrive, I went into my mom's bedroom where she was asleep, and I shook her lightly and told her that the day had arrived in which I had to have the money to turn in. What she did next would greatly surprise and hurt me deeply. When I asked her for the money, she said, "Get out of here, bitch, I don't have your damn money. Go to school, whore." (That one really hurt because unlike several of my friends, I was still a virgin at that time, and she smacked me so hard that I wore her handprint on my light-complexioned face for the first three periods of school that day.) It was just like a scene between her and my father, only she was my father this time. I guess we were back to "hurt people hurt others" unless the cycle was broken, and I vowed to do that! When I arrived at school, I went to Mr. Morris that morning and attempted to make up an excuse as to why I didn't have the money, {I'm sure he noticed the handprint on my face) and he just said, "Don't worry about it, it'll be okay. "I rushed off to my first period class. I guess he covered it for me. God bless him!

My senior year came around, and I only needed one credit to graduate, and that was my first period English class, but since I had no car and no way of leaving campus to go to a job, I was still reigning president of the

Library Club, a member of the National Honor Society, Who's Who in Academics as well as Who's Who in Music, a library aide, an office aide, and an aide to a couple of Mr. Morris' other band classes.

By the time I graduated from high school, I not only was graduating in the top ten academically of my high school class of nearly four hundred, but I also received the highest award in our school's band program, which was the Band Directors Award! I was on a roll that year; my parents even made it to the Band Awards banquet as well as to my graduation and presented me with a dozen yellow roses after graduation. By determination and the Grace of God, In spite of my dad moving us to Leavenworth, Kansas, nearly halfway through my junior year of high school (the only thing that made that time more tolerable were the wonderful friends and peers, I made in Leavenworth, including George, Roderick, Sherry, Tracey, Gary, Ramone, Mary, and Katrina) then turning around and moving us right back home less than one year later-a few months into my senior year of high school which caused me to miss senior pictures at both schools the one year that I had worked my behind off and saved $125.00 for the yearbook but had no photos of me.

The only other time I had the money to purchase a yearbook was in tenth grade, but evil, Tameka from my typing class stole it from me and she and her pitiful side-kick laughed about it, I guess they were hurt people hurting others or just plain mean. I'm leaning towards the latter. I'm sure sometime in both of their lives there were consequences for their cruel actions, but I felt like I was the one being punished by not being included in either school's yearbook (precious senior memories), my dad's ridiculous move also made me miss critical application deadlines for scholarships back home in which most had to be applied for during the summer before senior year. Yet I had somehow even with late submissions, received several scholarships to different universities and colleges in both Tennessee, Kentucky and Kansas, but due to not having the money for books or transportation to commute or per-mission to live in the dorms, I went to college in my own hometown in which I still had to bum a ride to class every day with fellow neighborhood friends. Our city had not developed a transit system yet and that surely would have made things a lot easier, but I would always tried to chip in for gas. Ironically, my dad would eventually go to drive for the transit system when it came to our town, but I was married and on my way to becoming a mom by then. Yes, in that order I am proud to say!

I got used to looking for rides, but it was extremely chal-lenging sometimes especially in the cold winters or inclem-ent weather getting across one end of the campus to another in enough time for my next class. There were no shuttles offered. Thursdays were usually the hardest for me because I only had one class on those days even though I carried a full load, I had to stay on campus all day long and wait for my ride to finish his classes in order to get home. Oh well, at least I got a lot of study time in. When I had asked my father for a car and thought for sure I would be rewarded for all my achievements, he told me that he had signed for too many cars for three siblings before and could not help me out, only not in such nice words as those! I believe his exact words were, "I don't a f-cking thing for you/my own kids, because I've given everything to the older ones!"

Asking for rides had become second nature to me as working at Krystal's after classes, and sometimes, my dad would give me a ride if he was home. I always had to pay a coworker to take me home because I got off well after midnight most nights, and my dad was already asleep. Also at age sixteen, I had started working for the military base's summer work program in which I worked with adults in very prestigious jobs and gained a ton of helpful knowledge and experience that really beefed up my resume. Oftentimes, they would take turns picking me up and giving me a ride home since I lived very close to the base. One year, I ended up working at the Comptroller's Office on the military base and my supervisor, Ms. Juanita, was so impressed that she told me to look her up after I graduated high school, and she could guarantee me a position there. I really loved that job and my coworkers. They nicknamed me teeny bopper since I was so young and they were all adults. I bonded with a deaf coworker named Candy and she would often come and pick me up and we'd go out to eat or the movies or something. She could read lips and taught me sign language. I wasn't quite as nervous about her coming over to my house, because if things did "pop off" between my parents, with her not being able to hear, I had time to make up an excuse for us to leave.

Yes, my memory was intact. I didn't know whether to rejoice or cry.

Though it had been only a split second or two, it felt like I had been away for decades, and then I heard the therapist repeat the question. I just told her that my earliest memory was my birthday party at age 4…without mentioning the drama. In a split second, I was right back to the present July 28, 2010, and realized where I was and why.

She went on reading, and she said she was going to perform a series of tests to determine where I was with everything so that she could map out a recovery routine and plan for me. She told me that I would be in the hospital for at least seven or eight days, and then she said possibly longer due to the difficulty I might have speaking once the pain meds for the severely fractured jaw and sawed open skull wore off. She went on to ask me questions about my home for aftercare once I was discharged.

Therapist: Will there be times in which you will be alone in your home immediately following your discharge?

Me: Yes, my husband has to return to work as well as my son, and our daughter will be getting ready to start her senior year in high school.

Therapist: So are there stairs in your home, and if so, how many?

Me: Yes, there are seventeen or eighteen stairs. All the bedrooms are upstairs, so I will only have to go down the stairs to access the kitchen and all exit doors.

Therapist: So you don't have any family or anyone who can be with you your first week or so to help you after you are discharged?

Me: (Feeling ashamed) I have three sisters and three brothers, but I'm pretty sure they will not be there for me. (Boy, was I right-not one would ever come up. It was close to another year before my dad and younger brother "passed through". None of my three (now late) sisters ever came to help me bathe, make me a meal or even a sandwich! My husband ended up putting a college dorm fridge next to my side of the bed and stocked it with juice boxes, lunchables, etc. so I wouldn't risk tackling the stairs and sustaining injury or death.)

Therapist: Well, I am sure that will add some time to your hospital stay. Due to liability reasons, we cannot discharge you until you prove that you can comfortably and competently conquer stairs on your own.

Me: Well, let's go!

Therapist: (Giggling) Yeah right.

Me: Let's Go!!

Therapist: Honey, I cannot allow you to attempt stairs less than twenty-four hours out of fifteen-hour brain surgery.

Me: LET'S GO!!!

My husband stated, "I think you should listen to my wife. I know it sounds crazy, but she is an amazingly strong woman, and I have witnessed her do amazing things after really invasive procedures, accidents, etc."

The therapist responded, "Well, let's get through the rest of these questions and tests, and we'll see.

After completion of the questions and further tests, I told her I was ready to try the stairs. Against her better judgment, she called for two orderlies. I was wheeled to the back staircase on my floor, and with an orderly on each side, her in front of me, and my husband behind me (of course, the Good Lord guiding me), I went up and down that steel staircase not once, not even twice, but an incredible four times without stumbling or having to hold on to anyone (but God's unchanging hand) for support. This was the very next day after an exhausting, intrusive and miraculous 15 hour brain surgery and blood transfusion! ***NOT Unto Death!***

All involved were blown away especially when the doctor came in later that night and read that huge accomplishment on my chart!

Needless to say, my hospital stay was not increased; in fact, it was decreased to five days instead of what was originally thought to be seven or eight days or even, at one time, a projected fourteen days or more minimum! ***NOT Unto Death!***

Chapter 21

Over the next couple months, the enemy came for me. He came for me **hard**! I suffered four more hospital stays due to post-op infections. Each time diagnosed as pockets of infection in one or more of the areas in which my jawbone had to be broken to fully extract the tumor.

The enemy came for me in other ways too: mainly depression. I often even had thoughts of suicide early on, I had been used to living a very active lifestyle, working and socializing. Now I was in horrendous pain most days and home alone until my daughter got home from school or my husband from his then horrible job.

Neurosurgeons are not allowed to prescribe "at home" pain medications and every other doctor or specialist that I saw did not know what to do for me. Again this had been something extremely rare and about 20 years earlier I had to have my wisdom teeth cut out and had a horrible reaction to the Percocets that I were prescribed, so it was pretty much noted in my charts to not give me anything which contained codeine. An old primary doctor of mine was left with the task of managing my pain and things went from bad to worse when he attempted the use of a fentanyl patch. It was too high of a dose and it had to be replaced every 3 days. About two weeks in, I showered and forgot to replace the patch. That sent me into a manic state in which I felt I had lost my mind and no one knew what was wrong with me. After a night from hell, I returned to that Primary Care doctor and he realized what had happened and gave me a referral to a pain management clinic.

That was one of the most horrible and humiliating experiences that I had ever encountered! All of my records to include the 75 pages of surgical notes, copies of all other relevant records, insurance information as well as photocopies of my driver's license and military dependent Identification had been sent prior to my appointment. I pushed through the pain, showered, dressed and even styled my hair nicely to cover most of the scar in my head and I only put a little lipstick on and nothing else on my face so that the scar and swelling along the jawline was still visible.

My husband took off from work and drove me to the appointment. Upon arrival they took my insurance card and photo IDs to make copies of. I filled out more paperwork and then my name was called to come back to begin my assessment. As my husband got up to accompany me, they rudely told him to remain seated and they would send for him if needed. I gave him a kiss and told him that I would be fine. Boy was I wrong!!!!!

When I got to the back the inquisition and badgering began! As I looked on in utter shock and amazement the hateful representative began to grill me. She asked why I was there and seeing that she had my records in her hand, I still respectfully answered her questions and told her all about the brain cancer journey. I also told her that it had been difficult to find the right pain medication to help with the four types of pain I was experiencing: hot sharp pains in the scalp which sometimes led to blisters, dull aching pain in the right side of my head where bone was removed and was now sinking in, as well as the electrical shocks that went down the right side of my face where my jaw had been broken in numerous places in order to successfully extract all of the tumor as well as the fierce and frequent headaches/migraine that were coming in clusters and lasting for days sometimes. I even went on to show her the records that I had brought from my Orthopedic doctors from being hit full frontal head on a few years earlier, in which case even with over fourteen fractures I opted for physical therapy to heal the 3 breaks in my right arm as well as the bones in my left foot. I also showed her that I did that with all of my ribs on my right side being fractured. She asked about other things in my life that may have warranted medication, I spoke of the 19 hour induced labor of my firstborn with nothing for pain as well as nothing for pain with my second child, and of course the gallbladder surgery I had shortly after delivering my first child and was unable to take anything strong because I was working and raising my son mostly by myself until my husband's tour of duty was concluded in our first tour to Germany. She said that my records said that I couldn't take percocets and I told her what had happened when I was given them following dental surgery 20 years earlier! She just scarfed and said something to the effect that I seemed well put together that day so what was I using or was I really feeling any pain? I told her that it took a lot of effort for me to pull myself together and come to this appointment. She continued to look at me in a rude and non-trusting manner. She said these pictures I was sent show the scars that were made, but I don't see them on you now. I told her that if she came closer that she could observe the scar down my jawline and that most of the scar that I incurred with the craniotomy was now covered with my hair in which I went through a lot of effort to style and cover it. I told her that even when I went back 2 weeks after the surgery to get the staples removed, I had pictures that showed that my hair was already growing into and over the staples.

The next thing I remember was her leaping up from her chair and coming over to me with no gloves or warning and holding and forcefully turning my face to observe the scar down my face. She then said, I only see a small area of the scar on my forehead and I once again explained that the rest was covered with my hair, but the pictures she had in my files showed the angle and length to which I was cut. Then, it happened! She looked at me with the most evil eyes I had ever seen and began yanking the clips and hairpins out of my hair and sifting through it like wheat! Between the pain I had already been experiencing and now the pain of her yanking and pulling sections of my hair apart, I screamed! Someone from the outside desk came and opened the door and I ran out looking like a "hot mess" with my once put together updo in total disarray. I ran to my husband sobbing uncontrollably and telling him to get me out of there! I now know why she didn't want my husband back there with me because he would have never tolerated or allowed her cruel behavior towards me! She was strategically placed there to "break me" and sadly she was successful that day, but it was **NOT Unto Death**. My husband filed a formal complaint with the clinic as well as with my then primary care doctor who had referred me. My doctor's office apologized and said they would refer me to another pain clinic. I told him that I would never set foot in one of those places again and I meant it!

When I was able to stop crying, I told my husband verbatim everything that had transpired. I remember him clenching his fists and punching the steering wheel a few times and yelling! He got out of the vehicle and paced around it a few times and then opened my car door and gently pulled me out of the vehicle and just embraced me as I began to sob again. It hurt me so much to see him break down like that because I knew this had been incredibly hard on him and I hated to see him so broken. I felt like such a burden. He asked if I wanted to go eat and I said, "look at my hair!" He said that I was still beautiful and that if I didn't want to eat inside, then we could pick up something and take it home. I told him that I just wanted to go home. He got me home and comfortable and then said he was going to pick me up something to eat. I laid in bed contemplating suicide! That was an evil spirit that kept coming to me throughout various times and events in my life, but God and my faith along with the prayers of the righteous were stronger and therefore, **NOT Unto Death***!*

Within an hour he was back with 2 different types of soup from my favorite soup place and a dozen of hot glazed doughnuts that I loved. He had grabbed himself a burger and we ate in bed, watched tv and he embraced me as we both napped off and on for the remainder of the day.

A few months later I was referred to a neurologist for an attempt to manage the pain and all I had been taking were Aleve and Excedrin Migraine. That neurologist did labs and stated that some of my counts were low and prescribed iron to bring my counts up and prescription strength naproxen for pain.

One afternoon my daughter checked in on me before going to work. I told her that I was okay and then I felt and tasted something in my mouth, kind of like when you have acid reflux. I went to spit in the toilet of my master bath and noticed it was pinkish in color, like I had drunk fruit punch or something like that, I told my daughter to have a good day at work and went to lay down. My energy had been pretty much non-existent lately. I had been hitting the prescription strength naproxen 3 - 4 times a day for a few weeks not realizing that I would soon regret taking something so common,

Around 8:45 that night, a sharp pain hit my stomach and I got out of bed in a panic to get to the toilet because I knew I felt a strong urge to throw up. In my haste, I left my cell phone on the bed. I lifted the toilet seat and started throwing up pure blood...my mouth tasted like "rusty nails" and then I had a pain hit me in my bottom. I immediately let the lid down and sat on the toilet to do what I thought was defecate. Instead, blood started flowing from my behind. It sounded like someone had turned on the water faucet. As I was sitting on the toilet waiting for it to stop, I felt the urge to throw up again. So now, I'm sitting on the toilet holding the trash can and blood is projecting from both my mouth and butt. I must have fallen off the toilet and had crawled halfway from the bathroom towards the bedroom to retrieve my phone but blacked out. The next thing I remember was the sound of voices and seeing flashing lights.

Apparently my husband had been trying to call me on his way home from work like he always did and still does but was getting no answer. I awoke in the hospital and looked around in confusion. I saw a nurse go running to get a doctor who I later learned was the **number one rated** gastrointestinal doctor in the area who just **happened** to be on call that night of all nights!

He came in and introduced himself and said that I had given everyone quite the scare. As he was talking my husband entered the room and kissed my forehead and held my hand as the doctor went on to say that I was brought in by ambulance with severe bleeding and in and out of consciousness. He said that my husband came home and found me on the floor bleeding out and called 911. My husband interjected and said, it looked like a crime scene and he didn't know what to think. The doctor began speaking again and said that the ambulance attendants took pictures of the scene (I bet those were the voices and flashing lights I vaguely recalled) as they prepared me for immediate transport. When I arrived, he had been shown the photos and observed that I was still bleeding out and asked if anyone was there with me. He continued speaking and advised that he went to the waiting area and spoke with my husband and this is what was said: "Your wife is obviously bleeding from an internal source. Judging by the pictures I was shown in conjunction with the amount of blood you were still losing, I told your husband that we needed to find the source of the bleeding before we could even consider a transfusion, but the issue would now be that the odds of you coming out from under the necessary anesthesia were slim to none, so I told him he would have to sign a release stating that he understood the risks before I could continue. Your husband said, "Save my wife! Where do I sign?" With that being said, we put you under and scoped you and realized that you had a couple of intestinal tears and judging by your medication list that is in our system, I believe the obvious culprit is the prescription strength naproxen. I repaired the tears and you are now getting a blood transfusion of a little over 5 units! (The average female has 7 to 8 units total) You lost about ⅔ of your body's total blood supply! I've heard about the journey you've been on as of recently and you are quite the fighter!" Thank you Lord that this too was **NOT Unto Death**!

My daughter entered the room with some clothing items and my cell phone and kissed me. I saw where I had numerous missed calls that were mostly my husband and daughter. As I was looking through the phone my two good friends and fellow Steeler buddies Eric Turner who was with Dorian Hunt were calling. I answered and told them I was just out of emergency surgery and in recovery. Within the hour (around 2am) they were both standing at the foot of my bed even though they both had to be at work in a matter of hours. I will *never* forget their act of kindness! It touched my husband as well.

Over the next several months, I was confined to my home mostly alone. No siblings nor my father or stepmother ever came to my home and visited me. However, I will never forget how my first cousin Michelle Koester, living in Louisiana, and her two daughters, who were all living in different states, drove all the way to our home in Tennessee and made Thanksgiving dinner for us all. I will always love them for that incredible act of selflessness. To this day, my kids often speak of it as the best Thanksgiving ever. Another cousin of mine named Darlene Smith and her husband, Carl, and her brother, Larnelle, drove up the following year to check on me. They are a little older than my husband and I. We truly appreciated the effort. They stayed with us for a couple of days and reminisced on good childhood memories. She and her brother were blown away at how far back my memories went as we spoke of happier times when I got to visit them on the farm as a young child. We had a wonderful visit, and she continues to check on me now.

I am also grateful to former coworkers/church family members Paulette Sizemore and Charla Canaday and their incredible family, who put on a charity concert event in which all money they took in was gifted to my family. God bless them; we really needed that money!

Of course, after completing my cancer treatment nine months later, I was surprised that when I arrived back at the airport in Knoxville that my dad was waiting with my husband and daughter, that was until I found out he was returning from seeing his mother in Charlotte, North Carolina, and he had taken a bus into Knoxville from Charlotte to await the arrival of my youngest brother to come and pick him up and drive him the remainder of the distance back to Clarksville.

Minutes after my brother's arrival, before he could even exit his car, the sky opened up and released a hailstorm like I've never seen that really damaged his car and made it necessary for him and my dad to stay until the next morning. To this day, my brother still thinks that overnight stay constitutes checking on me (nearly a year after the surgery and only the day after I finished cancer treatment). My husband used to joke and say about their visit and the hail storm, "Well, hell didn't have to completely freeze over!"

I was still able to continue paying and juggling our bills and finances, and my husband was working incredibly hard. I had even taken the laptop to Texas with me and continued paying bills, making calls and handling all financial matters during my two months of living in a hotel and going through cancer treatment by myself.

Again, I would always try to hide my worries and problems from him. I recall one day during my recovery, my husband came home from work, and when he entered the house, he called for me to come down the stairs. I thought he was testing me and his orders for me not to attempt the stairs, so I didn't come at first. He then called out to me again, and I said, "No, you told me not to take the stairs on my own." He said that it was okay. He would be watching me as I held on tightly to the banister and rails and carefully proceeded down the seventeen stairs.

When I got about three stairs from the bottom, he told me to sit down, close my eyes, and hold out my hands. I did just that. He then turned my hands outwards as if I was trying to guide myself in the dark, because I had them held out like someone who was about to have someone placed in them. What he did and said next will forever convince me that there is a God who reigns above and watches over us: He said, "With your eyes closed, can you physically see what is stressing you out and keeping you from recovering?" I replied, "No."

He then asked, "With your hands outstretched, can you physically touch those things that are stressing you out or preventing your full recovery?"

Once again, I replied, "No."

He then said, "Then it's not yours to bear!"

My mind was blown, my heart was pierced, and immediately, such a peace came over me.

My husband never speaks in that manner. Once again, God was confirming His presence and telling me that the hardships, pain, and other challenges that were current, as well as those that were yet to come, were ***NOT Unto Death***!

None of my husband's family ever came or offered to help either. They, to this day (almost thirty-nine years of marriage), have never been accepting of me or our two children because my husband did not marry traditionally, meaning I am neither full Puerto Rican nor Catholic.

The bills were mounting up because we had lost nearly two-thirds of our income by me not being able to return to work. The military still had not reimbursed us one cent! We had made several trips (500+ miles) round trip to the hospital for consultations, surgeries, post-op infections, tests etc. They owed us for gas, food and lodging. We even had one of our vehicles repossessed, and our home was facing foreclosure. Oh yeah, my cancer treatment was coming up in the upcoming months. The only place that offered the proton therapy (which that tumor responded to) was all the way in Houston, Texas. The American Cancer Society and other charities would yet again deny me assistance, stating there was a one-year waiting list. If only we could predict when we would have cancer and when, if, or where treatment would be. It would be even better if there weren't so many people diagnosed with cancer. Not one family member was about to reach into their pockets and offer a dime!

I needed airfare to Houston plus money to live in a hotel for two months and meals while I underwent cancer treatment alone because my husband had to stay back in Tennessee and work and allow our daughter to complete her senior year in high school.

One day our doorbell rang and in came our neighbors at the time Chad and Rebecca. They told us that they had been talking and trying to figure out a way to bless and then handed us an envelope. My husband opened it and to our surprise there was a round-trip ticket (open end date) to Houston. That had been a great concern because again Tricare was refusing to pay in advance for my travel for cancer treatment, and my husband had already taken off work the month prior to drive me to Houston for my cancer consultation. God was using so many people to bless us!

That's okay, this month (April 2025), I am fourteen years and counting cancer free! Approaching fifteen years brain tumor free!

In other words, God showed up and showed out. The odds of getting that type of tumor was 1/16th of 1% of the entire world population. The odds of surviving the surgery were lower. The odds of living past 2 years was unheard of and I am 14+ years and counting. *NOT Unto Death!*

More eloquently and biblically put, this sickness was *NOT Unto Death*!

I was once told by a very special person in my life that God gives His most challenging battles to His strongest warriors or maybe to those who will give Him the glory as I hope I have done!

So as I reflect on the following:

- nearly dying twice while my mother was carrying me (*NOT Unto Death!*)
- being born prematurely in the '60s (*NOT Unto Death!*)
- nearly dying as a toddler from a major head injury (*NOT Unto Death!*)

- growing up in a very volatile, toxic, and dysfunctional home to say the least (***NOT Unto Death***!)
- having to live in a battered women's shelter along with an infant for weeks because of parental abuse (***NOT Unto Death***!)
- being hit full frontal head-on and sustaining fourteen fractures (***NOT Unto Death***!)
- of course, the extremely rare brain tumor/cancer (***NOT Unto Death***!)
- being told upon initial discovery/diagnosis of the brain tumor that no one could help me (***NOT Unto Death***!)
- living in a hotel in Houston for two months and going through thirty-five rounds of cancer treatment by myself (***NOT Unto Death***!)
- bleeding internally and unaware of it for days due to a medication that was prescribed by a former neurologist I use to see and losing nearly two thirds of my total blood supply (***NOT Unto Death***!)
- Rather than being helped, but instead treated like dirt under her shoe at a pain clinic (***NOT Unto Death***!)
- waking up to the sound of breaking teeth in my mouth, pieces of teeth, or an actual tooth being in my mouth (sustained from both the numerous fractures of the jaw and thirty-five rounds of radiation) yet being denied implants for nearly two

years (by the military insurance saying implants were cosmetic); even though my mouth would not open wide enough for a partial or plate and I was only 122 lbs. you could see every bone in my body and about to go on a feeding tube. (**NOT Unto Death**!)

- suffering from severe depression and feeling like a burden despite the amazing support and love I received from my husband and children- serious thoughts of suicide (**NOT Unto Death**!)

- my precious friend and hair braider, Dhyka, who did my hair a few times with a post-dated check in order to continue to make me feel beautiful, set up a GoFundMe page to help with the $64,000 estimate I received for implants and only she and one other friend, Wendy Knake, out of thousands of views/shares donating (**NOT Unto Death**!)

- The Second visit to "Dr Doom" in which he told me to be prepared to lose my right eye that was damaged during the brain surgery (**NOT Unto Death**!)

- losing all of my teeth or at least pieces of them on the right side of my mouth and refusing to leave home from embarrassment and writing count-less letters and pleading for help from cancer and other charities, talk shows, dentists, and doctors and even the facility in which the surgery was performed, etc. (***NOT Unto Death***!)

- getting down to a size 00 (with my 5'10" frame) and being able to see every bone in my body as I awaited an "exception to policy" (with the aid and perseverance of Congressman John Duncan Jr.'s Office of Knoxville, Tennessee intervening after I wrote to him. I can't thank them enough for their kindness and compassion for our military and their families.) With the military insurance before finally being approved just as I was about to go on a feeding tube (***NOT Unto Death***!)

- pretty much being told that I couldn't do/accomplish most of the things in my life to include writing this book (***NOT Unto Death***!)

It makes me feel that maybe that person who spoke of God giving His strongest battles to His strongest soldiers was correct. For it is now that I realize that my strength and faith ***always*** outweighed my weaknesses, diagnosis, environment, situations and challenges!

Thank You, Lord, for each and every day, and that these things were ***NOT unto Death***!

JUST A LITTLE SOMETHING EXTRA THAT GOD GAVE TO ME IN 18 MINUTES!

YOU MAY BE SEEING MORE THINGS LIKE THIS IN THE FUTURE (upcoming books)

I WOKE UP DEAD

This morning, I woke up dead
Recalling various events in my head
Regretting words that out of hurt or
anger that I may have said
Reminiscing and missing the things I use to dread
Something as simple as cleaning or making the bed
Wait a minute, it just hit me… it was all just a dream
So, I began to rejoice and smile with gleam
For God has given me another chance
to wipe the slate clean
Another day to repent and love the
good as I pray for the mean
A chance to be grateful even when
times and resources are lean
So tonight, when I lay down and close my eyes
Tomorrow, I pray that I will once again rise
To tell of God's goodness and rebuke the lies

So, during those times you think you
may have woken up dead
Remove the shackles, dance and be glad
That you really didn't wake up dead!

By: Lonnette Liggins Collazo

"My Life's Journey- Still in Progress and still NOT UNTO DEATH!"

"A few years after major childhood trauma."

(That's me outside front row and the rest of
me finally grew into those legs.)
"The BEST part of my childhood – BAND!"

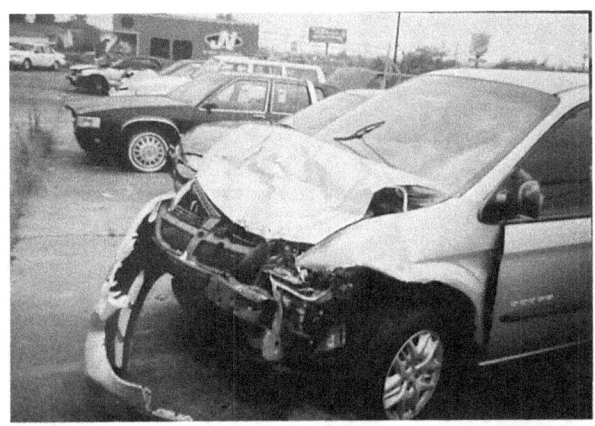

"Head On Collision – NOT UNTO DEATH!"

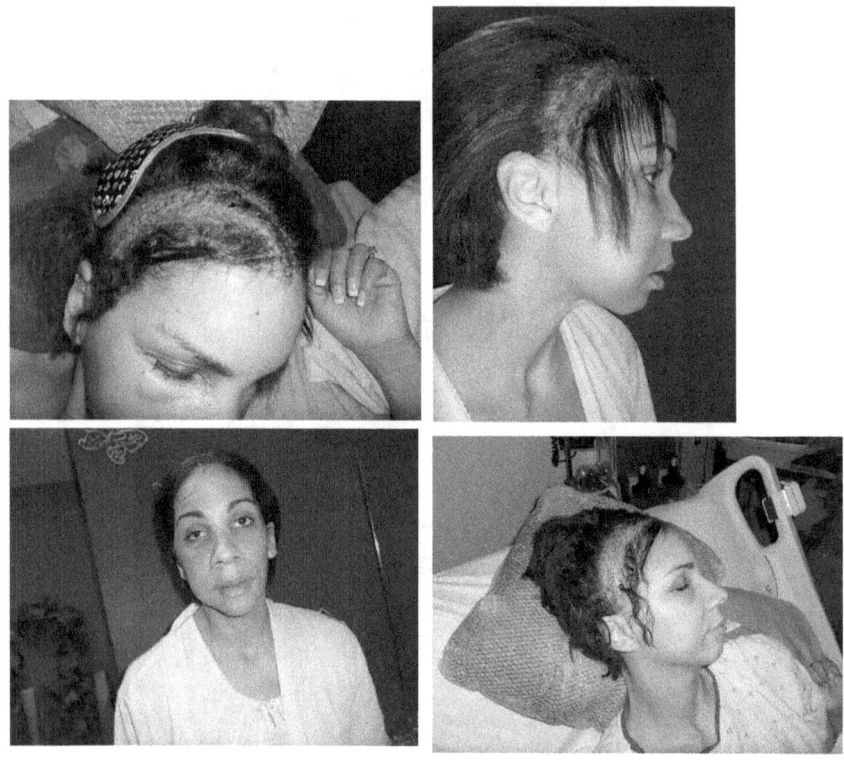

"Aftermath of my fifteen hour brain surgery."

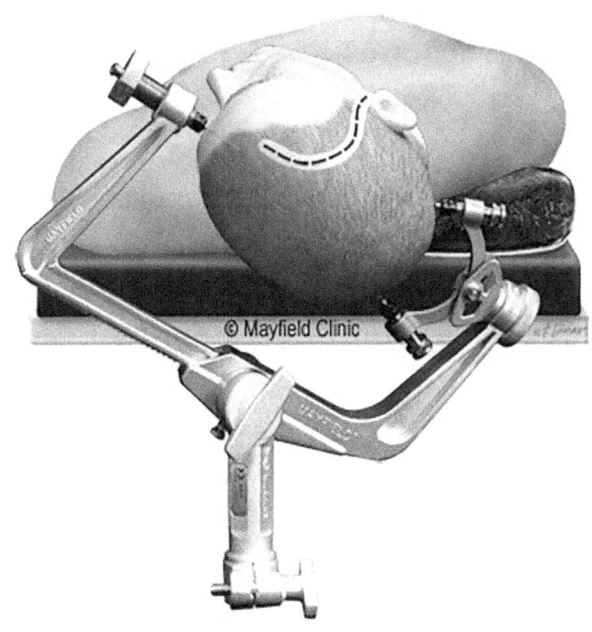

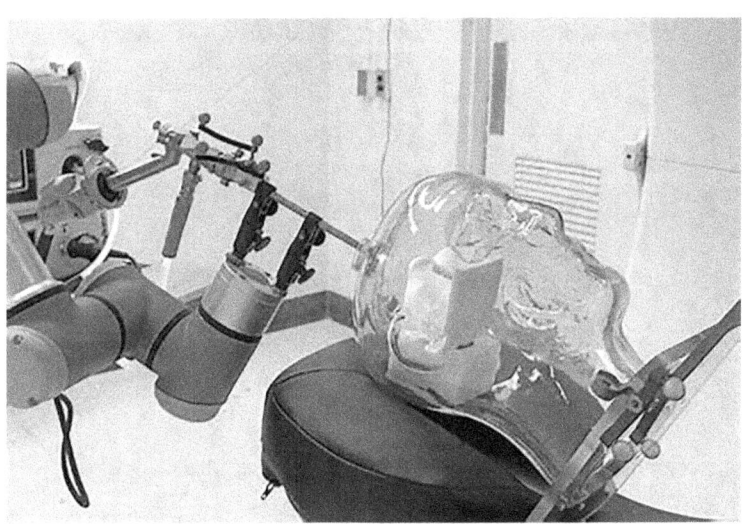

"Two of the devices used during my surgery."

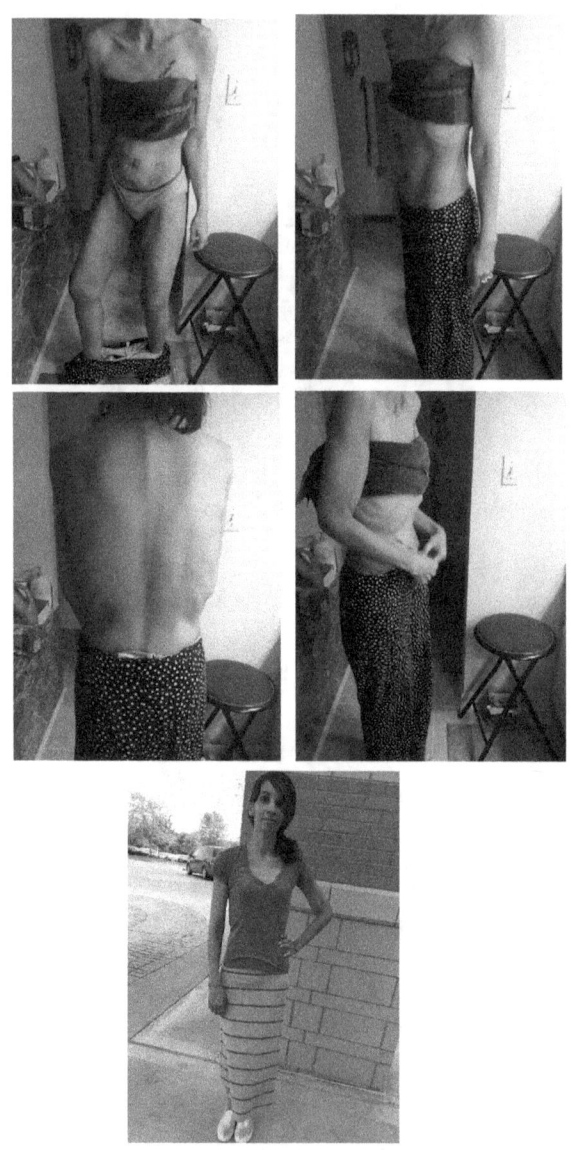

Me, at 5'10" and 122 pounds, fighting the military
insurance for dental implants to be able to eat
instead of going on permanent feeding tube.

"Before and after my dental implants."

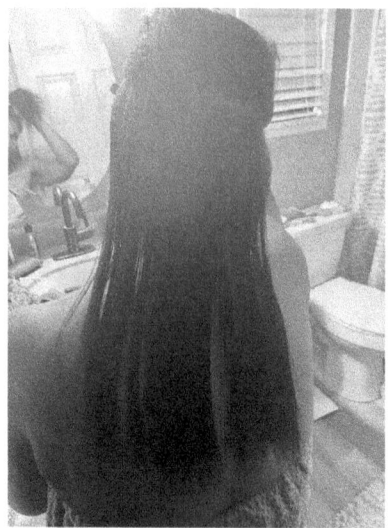

"Never lost hair after 35 rounds of Cancer Treatment or all the stress of every challenge it brought. In fact, it became thicker and longer"

"Two days out of my 3rd sinus surgery and finding out my dad had died two days before!"

"The Journey but still NOT UNTO DEATH!"

"The best part of my life is waking up next to my amazing, supportive hubby!"

"Hubby and I after purchasing a new home after living in a camper for 10 months."

"Our last Christmas post-surgery in our old home."

"Hubby and I at a festival- 13 years out from brain surgery."

"Hubby and I on our first cruise since brain surgery."

"Not only surviving but thriving."

"Healthy, Happy and Thriving in 2024- 14 years surviving."

About the Author

I am your average lady who has been dealt some "not so average" blows in life. I have faced many challenges in many areas such as: medical, financial, relationships, mental, physical, verbal and emotional abuse and there are certainly some more categories I could add.

After going through so many trials and challenges, at times I felt defeated. There were some cases I was told there was no hope of success or survival. In fact, things often felt very bleak.

One day, I had an epiphany: that maybe just maybe these things that I had experienced were not some sort of punishment, curse or even a result of anything I may have done.

Instead, I thought, just maybe it was for times such as these to encourage others. Perhaps this was my purpose in life: *"To go through so that I could help others get through!"* In other words, to encourage others and provide them with some hope when there seems to be none.

Afterall, from a child growing up in Church or listening to my grandparents, it had been instilled in me that we **all** have gifts and purposes in this earthly life. Personally, I believe that to be true and perhaps the biggest disappointment to ourselves and our "Higher Power" is never realizing what they are/were; even worse, knowing what they are and ignoring or giving up on them!

I believe that some of my gifts are perseverance, determination, patience and having faith. You know looking beyond the norm and negativity in an effort to find my inner peace and ability to succeed. As it's often referred to as, "turning the negatives into positives."

It hasn't always been easy or come easily to me. In fact, there have been several times in which I have just felt like just throwing up my hands and calling it quits! There were/are several people along my journey that have counted me out! That was/is their biggest mistake, misconception or transgression that they can commit towards me!

After over 5 decades it is now that I truly believe that my purpose is to acknowledge those gifts in conjunction with my life experiences and to use them to uplift and encourage not only myself but others as well.

As they say, "You can't have testimonies without tests" …right!?!

I also want to reiterate how important it is for you to make these doctors and medical personnel to do their job! No one knows your body better than you! If you know something is wrong and you can't get that doctor to listen to you, then move on to someone who will!

If you get told there is no hope or counted out along the way, remember God has the FINAL SAY!

www.ingramcontent.com/pod-product-compliance
Lightning Source LLC
Chambersburg PA
CBHW060455290526
45791CB00001B/123